HAWAII

A Walker's Guide
2nd Edition

HAWAII

A Walker's Guide
2nd Edition

Rod Smith

HUNTER
PUBLISHING INC

Hunter Publishing Inc.
300 Raritan Center Parkway
Edison NJ 08818
Tel (908) 225 1900
Fax (908) 417 0482

ISBN 1-55650-694-5

© 1995 Hunter Publishing Inc.

Cover photograph: *Na Pali Cliffs, Kauai*
by the author

Contents

Hawaii 155

Oahu

1

The View From Diamond Head

Distance from crater floor: 1.5 miles
Permit requirements: none
Rating: strenuous family

Diamond Head is probably the most famous view in the entire Pacific. It comes as a surprise to many visitors, however, to discover they can also hike up through the extinct volcano to the lookout at its crowning glory.

Along the way, you can see some of the most beautiful vistas in Hawaii and at its peak you will discover an unsurpassed panorama stretching all the way from Koko Head and Koko Crater to the romantic Leeward Coast, the scene for much of Julie Andrews' movie *Hawaii*.

Diamond Head is, in fact, the dominant feature of Waikiki, where most visitors spend at least part of their vacation. The volcanic crater, which has been extinct for 150,000 years, is only 800 feet tall and enthusiasts looking for a hearty walk or hike can climb to the top without much trouble.

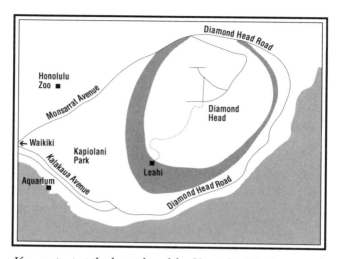

If you start at the base, head for Kapiolani Park, named for the wife of David Kalakaua, the last king of the Islands. On weekends, the park is a circus of community activity. Within its 140 acres are many attractions, including the Waikiki Aquarium. For many, the favorite is the paved biking, jogging and walking trail around the park perimeter, under the romantic hills of the volcano.

Kapiolani Park, large, flat and shady, is also the site of the Honolulu Zoo, which has been considerably improved in recent years. It is a major gathering place for Honolulu's vast army of runners; Honolulu is known to have one of the largest running populations of any city in the United States. On the first Sunday of each December, the park is the finish line for the Honolulu Marathon. This run has been attracting thousands since 1981 for its 26.2-mile run from the Aloha Tower downtown to Hawaii Kai and back to the park. Kalakaua Avenue and a shoreline string of new highrise apartment buildings and hotels border the park. The ironwood-lined avenue runs between the park and the buildings along the coast and becomes Diamond Head Road at the southern base of the volcano. From the parks along the road, there are splendid views of the sea.

To begin the climb, you can drive up Diamond Head Road into the crater floor, or head up the sidewalk out of Waikiki. You will be struck by the opulence of the homes built as retreats by businessmen in Honolulu.

The first sight along the way is the Diamond Head Lighthouse at the top of the rise. A steel-framed stone tower of glistening white, it was once Hawaii's grandest, making it safe to journey by sea across the Pacific.

Probably the most famous view before heading up into the crater comes at the Diamond Head Lookouts. Visitors can peer down at the sparkling water far below and the windsurfers jumping from wave to wave like tiny toy people. The view to the east embraces the lavish community on Black Point, which is where the likes of Claire Booth Luce and Doris Duke once lived. Above it all rise the mighty cliffs of Diamond Head, giving a clear impression of the enormity of the volcano.

Stay on Diamond Head Road, bearing left just past the lookouts, until you come to Fort Ruger. From there a sign will indicate your route up the narrow road. There is another lookout just before going into the carved tunnel leading to the crater floor. From here you can see Kahala, Honolulu's richest suburb, and the Kahala Hilton, birthplace of the Hawaiian Open and one of the best golf courses in the Pacific.

A hike from the floor of the crater to the peak is dry and hot, but the panorama offered from the summit is awesome. This climb is an absolute must for the entire family. Although a large part of the crater and the surrounding area are a military district, the hiking trail is under the jurisdiction of the Division of State Parks and is open to the public.

Extensive fortifications and tunnels for the fire control areas of the fort were built into the limestone and ash walls of this late Pleistocene volcanic cone. They are hard to see from the ground or air, but can be easily reached from the short trail beginning in the parking lot.

The volcano got its name in the early 1800s when British sailors found calcite crystals on the slopes of the crater and thought they had found diamonds. The "tuff" crater was then called Kaimana-Hila (Diamond Hills). Geologists speculate that the crater was formed by a violent steam explosion 100,000 years ago.

The trialhead on the southwest end of the parking lot is well marked and the trail is easy to follow to the summit. Kiawe trees, locally used to make charcoal, abound across the lower reaches of the crater, lending it a lush green color, except in the dry season.

There are railings along much of the trail as it climbs up the crater wall. There is also a beautiful view of the inside of the crater just past the first concrete lookout. Then the trail climbs up steep steps leading to a dark, angled tunnel. A flashlight is helpful, especially with children who may be frightened, but it is not necessary as light can soon be seen at the other end.

A steeper staircase with 99 steps leads hikers into a short tunnel, at the end of which an observation room offers the first view of Waikiki and greater Honolulu. To its right is an unlit, iron spiral staircase leading to the top bunker high over Waikiki. For the best views, come out through the bunker and continue the short climb to the very top of the fortifications atop the ancient volcano. There you will be struck by one of the finest views in all of Hawaii – one not many visitors get a chance to see and something you will never forget.

The magical beach at Waikiki and its modern steel and glass hotels are the first thing you will notice. Between them and the familiar tourist streets is the lush green of Kapiolani Park and the Waikiki Shell, a favorite spot for outdoor concerts all year round. The pink palace at the center of the beach is the Royal Hawaiian, the second oldest standing hotel in Waikiki. It was built in 1927 in a stucco, Mediterranean style, and is reminiscent of the days when the well-to-do came to Hawaii by ship and moved in with their steamer trunks to stay for weeks.

Beyond Waikiki, it is easy to make out another extinct volcano, Punchbowl, the National Cemetery of the Pacific, a favorite lookout for hikers. Behind it stand the incredibly lush Koolau Mountains with their Tantalus-Ualakaa Park. It takes strong hikers to reach them.

Children like to watch the giant aircraft land and take off from Honolulu International Airport. The outermost Reef Runway is a unique engineering wonder. Beyond it you can see the romantic Leeward Coast, the scene for Hawaii's most popular luau at Paradise Cove and some of the best hiking opportunities in the Islands.

Behind the coast stand the mighty Waianae Mountains, home of Schofield Barracks. Together with Pearl Harbor, which can be seen beyond the airport, they were the targets of the 1941 Japanese attack that began American involvement in World War II. Between the Waianae Mountains and Pearl Harbor under Schofield Barracks are the rich plains of central Oahu. It comes as a surprise to many, but these are still highly productive agricultural lands. At their feet lies the Diamond Head Lighthouse. The bizarre angle of this building also sometimes comes as a surprise.

Instead of a stark white monument standing against the azure blue sky, hikers making it to the very summit of the volcano see the lush green of its well-manicured lawns.

Back to the east is another sweeping view of Kahala, that ultra-class suburb where the elite of Honolulu and the entertainment world make their homes. Even from a distance, the palm trees can be seen swaying gently in the soft Pacific breezes. The beaches of Kahala are not particularly good for strolling, but the waters are favorites for wind boarding and surfing. This elevated lookout gives the best view of the reef that almost entirely rings Oahu. This natural barrier is responsible for the gentle surfs that help make this island so popular. The two hills in the distance are Koko Head and Koko Crater. The crater is the youngest volcano on the island, though it is quiet.

Koko Head is the backside of the semi-submerged volcano known as Hanauma Bay. That is where Elvis filmed *Blue Hawaii* and it hosts another great lookout, as well as three trails for hiking.

Just to the Honolulu side of the two volcanoes is Hawaii Kai. Another world-class suburb, this was the brain child of Henry J. Kaiser, an important developer in the Islands during the 1950s.

It is possible to hike completely around the rim of the crater and return to the parking lot by cutting through the brush, but the trail is steep and dangerous because of the loose volcanic rock and ash. Only the most experienced hikers should try it. Local residents familiar with the frequent stories about emergency helicopters having to pluck adventuresome visitors from the cliffs advise sticking strictly to the well-marked trail.

The trip back down to the floor of the crater along this main route bears no real surprises. For hikers heading back to town, it is possible to take a left at Diamond Head Road for a different route into Waikiki. This offers more views of many of the same sights, worth seeing for enthusiasts with the energy. It also takes you through Kaimuki, where you will see a more local side of island life than in the tourist meccas.

2

Walking Waikiki

Distance: 5-7 miles
Permit requirements: none
Rating: family

Waikiki beckons with gorgeous sand, dependable sunshine, first-class dining, international shopping, and splendid nightlife. Over a century ago, Robert Louis Stevenson wrote:

"If anyone desires such old fashioned things as scenery, quiet, pure air, clear sea water, heavenly sunsets hung out before his eyes over the Pacific and the distant hills of Waianae, recommend him to Sans Souci Beach."

It is still magic today. Sans Souci is the beach at Waikiki right under the cliffs of Diamond Head. Waikiki Beach itself is not one continuous crescent of sand, but a series of beaches, some natural and others manmade, each with its own ambience and habitués. The entire stretch is public and accessible by right of ways. You can walk on the sand and connecting sea walls all the way from Sans Souci to Kuhio Beach Park and Ft. DeRussy Beach.

In the early morning or the later afternoon and evening, you get the real sense of being on an island in the middle of the largest body of water in the world. At other times of the day, the beach is devoted largely to water-oriented activities of all kinds, though the tropical trade breezes make sure it is always comfortable. Several beaches "belong" to beachboys who take visitors on boat rides or give surfing lessons; others are home to outrigger canoes, catamarans, surfers, wind boarders, or boogie boarders. Most of the action on the beach takes place at Waikiki, but the entire strand offers rich and varied opportunities for hiking and walking.

Officially, Waikiki is a peninsula about one half-mile wide and two miles long, bounded by Diamond Head and the Ala Wai Canal. But, for those in search of a good hike, it stretches all the way from the Diamond Head Lighthouse to the Ala Wai boat harbor.

Most visitors spend at least part of their vacation at Waikiki. It is fashionable for many to compare it with Coney Island but, if that was ever valid, it no longer is today. Since 1986, Waikiki has undergone nearly $1 billion in private and public renovations and additions. With the increase in competition among visitor destinations worldwide, hotel operators and government officials have committed themselves to maintaining Waikiki as a leader.

The first glimpse most visitors get of Hawaii's most famous sand comes at Prince Kuhio Beach between the turn-of-the-century Moana Hotel and Kapahulu Avenue. It used to be marked by an enormous gateway arch, but that has disappeared in the name of progress.

You can rent surf boards at the Waikiki Beach Center across from the Hyatt Regency, or use it as an ideal starting point for a hike to see all this cosmopolitan resort has to offer. The principal street along the beach

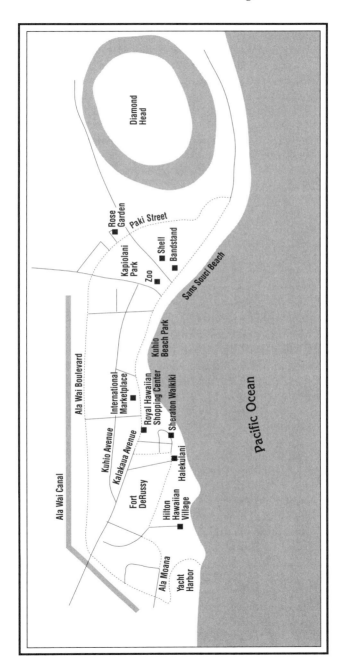

and its parks is Kalakaua Avenue, named for David Kalakaua, the last king of Hawaii.

Heading toward Diamond Head, visitors come to the Honolulu Zoo. Especially with the addition of an African safari landscape, it has been much improved in recent years – although it is still a long way from being an equal to the world-class zoos of Europe or the U.S. mainland.

There is a weekend art mart on the Diamond Head side of the zoo. You may get the impression it is little more than a casual sale of folk art, but it takes place every week and, if you compare local artwork sold elsewhere, you will find all prices here are at a premium.

Kapiolani Park sprawls over 170 acres between Kapahulu and the extinct crater. In addition to the zoo, it hosts an aquarium, tennis courts, a golf driving range, and an archery range. Most concerts in the park take place at the Waikiki Shell or the Kapiolani Bandstand. The bandstand is also the site of a weekly 7:30 a.m. Sunday marathon clinic, where doctors and health professionals offer sound advice for fitness enthusiasts. Back on Kalakaua Avenue, the most visible landmark is the new first class tennis complex.

The antique gold and green jewelry box nearby is the last trolley stand left from the turn of the century, when rails were the way to get around in Hawaii. Queens Surf and Sans Souci Beach across the street were popular with the haoli (white) businessmen and their families at that time and are still local favorites today.

Opened in 1904, the Waikiki Aquarium shares the beaches, and it is a wonderful state-owned collection of sealife with a reasonable entry fee. It has more than 300 species of Pacific marine life including giant clams, sharks, deep-water crustaceans, harbor seals, sea turtles, and saltwater crocodiles.

From the aquarium you should walk toward Diamond Head. Along the way, you will pass the Mrs. Walter F. Dillingham Memorial Fountain, named after one of the original grande dames of Hawaii.

At the intersection of Kapahulu, you have the option of continuing up to the Diamond Head Lighthouse or all the way up into the old volcano (Chapter 1). Alernatively, you can turn left to complete a loop around all or part of Waikiki. Heading toward the Ala Wai Canal, the path leads through the shade of some great banyan trees, which make it an ideal spot for picnicking.

On Paki Street behind the zoo and on the way to the Ala Wai Canal, you will discover one of Waikiki's most closely guarded secrets, the Kapiolani Rose Garden. Its blooms are fed with such exotic fertilizers as giraffe dung. There is no fee and its flowers are always in bloom, which makes it a picnicking hot spot.

The Ala Wai Canal and its broad promenade stretch along the backside of Waikiki from Kapahulu to the marina. It was dredged in the 1920s to drain the surrounding swamps and duck ponds and to carry runoff from the streams that often flooded Waikiki. But the ultimate result was to create today's solid land mass out of what had been a swamp. Early in the morning or late in the afternoon, a lot of residents jog or walk around the canal's promenade and in the afternoon there are usually kayakers skimming along the water to stay in shape. At sunset, the sky turns glorious shades of red, with Diamond Head to your back and Punchbowl and the Koolau Mountains on the side away from the sea.

The canal and its promenade deadhead at the Ala Wai Yacht Harbor, haven for more than 1,000 private boats

– with no commercial vessels allowed. There are long waiting lists here.

The most pleasant walk back is by the sea. The beach edges past the Hilton Lagoon at its Hawaiian Village and on past Ft. DeRussy toward Diamond Head. The military post is maintained much like a park, but the real treat here is the swimming. The Army Corps of Engineers has excavated an enormous in-the-ocean pool by removing blocks of coral, and two giant rafts create a unique place for swimming where the waters are always warm and calm.

The park is also the site of the Army Museum, headquartered in the old coastal artillery battery building. It looks like a war ruin because the military tried to demolish the structure with everything in it, but the bunker proved too solid to crush. Blowing it up would have blown all the windows out of the nearby high rises, so it was left.

The ultra-class Halekulani Hotel preserves the oldest shred of old Hawaii in its 1917 "House Without a Key," site of the original Charlie Chan detective novel. It is still a great place for a stroll or a snack, with a smashing view of Diamond Head.

Back on Kalakaua, you can keep on walking through the Royal Hawaiian Shopping Center. Its four floors of shops are a magnet for Japanese tourists. The Sheraton Waikiki, Royal Hawaiian, and Moana Hotels all sit in its lap and they are landmarks of different vintages.

Sheltered under enormous banyans, the International Marketplace is another shopping favorite. And back at the center of the beach, King's Alley completes the collection of Waikiki shopping arcades for strolling.

Mainland visitors to Hawaii tend to wake up early, and they all revel in the sunsets. Whatever time you do it, strolling about Waikiki will give you a good idea why millions have found it a very special place.

3

Hanauma Bay

Hanauma Bay, as everyone knows who has visited Hawaii, is another popular lookout on Oahu. It offers three well-marked hiking trails, although its main attraction is the rare sealife sanctuary where the fish are so unaccustomed to human predators they will eat bread from visitors' hands.

Hanauma is known as the site for Elvis Presley's movie *Blue Hawaii*. The name means "curved bay" in Hawaiian, and it is one of the most popular spots in the Islands for snorkeling and watching the tropical fish, but the views themselves are well worth the trip. The bay is really an extinct volcanic crater with one side washed away and exposed to the vast blue Pacific. It is such a romantic setting that it was also the site for the unforgettable love scene with Burt Lancaster and Deborah Kerr in *From Here to Eternity*.

Sitting high above on the lookout at the end of one of the hiking trails, you can see the turquoise water below, with snorkelers everywhere feeding the fish, and other visitors just relaxing and sun bathing in the warm tropical breeze.

Some kama'ainas (islanders) claim the best view is the short hike up Koko Head, which is marked at the Hanauma Bay lookout. Others claim that the best way to see this beautiful spot is to hike around the waters to the left of the park along a rock ledge for a sea-level perspective.

You can have a lot of fun out of the water, but if you decide you want to see the incredibly colorful fish, you can rent any equipment needed at the concession in the center of the beach. Take some bread or toast, or, better yet, some frozen peas. They are favorite snacks for the local fish, and visitors with masks – their own or rented - will feel a little like Dame Edith Evans as the bird lady in *Mary Poppins* when all the fish come swimming around their legs at Hanauma.

KOKO HEAD TRAIL
Distance: 1 mile
Permit requirements: none
Difficulty: family

It is prudent for the protection of your car (and for convenience) to park in the lot at the end of the bay road overlooking Hanauma Bay. First-time visitors will want to spend a little time walking over to the lookout at the head of the trail down to the beach and catch another glimpse of the astonishing view.

To reach the trail itself, walk back up to the highway you drove out on. There is a gate across a paved road on the left side back toward Diamond Head and Waikiki which keeps vehicles from driving to the summit of Koko Head, the extinct volcanic rim enclosing Hanauma Bay. It is easy to walk around the gate for the short hike to the peak. The trail beckons with a rich geological tapestry and wonderful views of the bay and beautiful coastline.

Koko Head is a 640-foot "tuff cone," and legend has it that it is the last place on Oahu where the volcano goddess, Pele, made a home for herself. From its peak, there are enchanting views northeast to Koko Crater and the Monterey-like coastline around Hanauma Bay. There are also outstanding vistas of Diamond Head back by Waikiki, Hawaii Kai (the 6,000-acre development that was industrialist Henry J. Kaiser's last project), and the languid Koolau Mountains slicing the island of Oahu in half from the Leeward to the Windward Coasts.

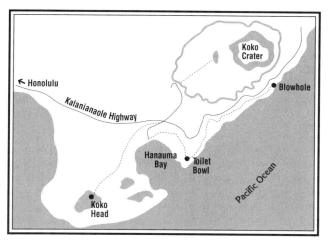

Two little craters below the summit away from town, Nonolula and Iheihalauakea, are also in view. On a clear day one of the best spectacles is the island of Molokai 200 miles across the channel, where humpback whales sing and cavort.

It is possible to return to the bay by crossing the two little craters. There is no trail, however, and the slopes of the craters are steep, the surface is loose, and the hike can be dangerous.

FROM THE BAY
TO THE BLOWHOLE

Distance: 2 miles

Permit requirements: none

Difficulty: strenuous family

Hanauma Bay was made a marine life conservation district in 1967. That means catching or injuring sea life is prohibited. As a result, it is a delightful place to explore tidepools or to snorkel and discover the extravagant underwater life.

It is easy to hike the shelf above the waterline from the beach along the east side of the bay. But you should watch out for the tidepools and be careful of the waves which can crash onto the ledge.

The most popular sight along the trail is "Toilet Bowl" just beyond the far end of the bay. This unusual spot is really a hole about 30 feet around and 10 feet deep, which is alternately filled and drained from below as waves come in and recede. Swimmers can jump or slide into the pool as it empties, and they scramble out when the bowl fills. On the other side of the bay (from Toilet Bowl) is an area called "Witches' Brew." It is prudent to avoid this western side of the bay toward town, because of the considerable turbulence. The waves can be dangerous and there is a strong undertow.

The climb from "Toilet Bowl" to the ridge overlooking the famous bay is an easy one; or you can follow the coast around Palea Point. From there to the Blowhole, you will see a lot of local people snorkeling and fishing. The people here are friendly; a wave and a smile will win friends – and maybe a free fish for lunch.

After a mile or so, the ledge above the water becomes narrow, and a degree of agility is required to climb and jump over the lava while avoiding the crashing waves. A safer approach is along the side of the road. Not for the fainthearted, the water-level route can be exciting. But the views of Maui, Lanai and Molokai from the roadway are reminiscent of the magic Bali Hai scenes of *South Pacific* – as the clouds gather around the peak of Haleakala, the House of the Sun, rising 10,000 feet above Maui.

The Holona BIowhole is a narrow lava vent through which the sea surges as the waves come in and go out. Its geysers spray 30 to 50 feet into the air, depending on the tide and surf. It is a delightful end to a beautiful hike. But, for the more timid, it is just as easily visited bv car.

KOKO CRATER TRAIL
Distance: 1 mile
Permit requirements: none
Difficulty: strenuous

To reach the beginning of this trail from Hanauma Bay, you can take the road opposite the entrance to the bay road by the sign marked "Aloha Hawaii Job Corps Training Center." A half-mile beyond the main office there is an abandoned railroad incline that leads directly up to the summit with its spectacular views. The railroad ties that have been left behind make it an easy climb. Portions of the track are overgrown, however, so it calls for a little climbing dexterity. It is especially important to be careful on the trestle that corsses a gulch on the way up. Caution has to be exercised again on the platform at the peak because the wood is rotten and broken in a number of places.

The panoramic views from the powerhouse and 1,200-foot lookout are astonishing. Looking out in every direction, you can take in the sweep of the Koolau Mountains to the north, Diamond Head and the ritzy neighborhoods of Hawaii Kai and Kahala to the west, and Koko Head and Hanauma Bay at your feet. The scene makes the climb well worth the effort and it is a spectacular spot for picnicking. The crater itself houses a botanical garden and bridle paths for riders.

You can drive to Hanauma Bay for the day of hiking or take the public bus from Kalakaua and Montsarrat Streets in Waikiki during summer months. For the truly energetic, it is also possible to walk it – about 10 miles, along the street called Kalanianaole Highway.

4

The Pali Lookout

After the view from Diamond Head, the Pali Lookout (also called the Nuuanu Pali) is probably the most spectacular panorama in the Pacific – certainly on Oahu. Residents and experienced visitors alike rate the lookout high on their list of the most awesome sights in the Islands. The Pali Lookout takes in a breathtaking sweep of landscapes seemingly stretching all the way up the Windward Coast of the island. In particular, the cool uplands host the lush tropical rainforests of Windward Oahu – a real surprise for visitors expecting beaches, but not much more. All the colors of the rainbow play against lush vegetation on sheer cliffs dropping to the sea below. The sweeping vista may be the most amazing scene this side of Shangri La.

The lookout itself is in a crack eroded by wind and rain in the Koolau Mountains. The tradewinds rush through with such force that visitors often have to brace themselves to stay upright. Hang on, because this is one place where a lot of things blow away, from eye glasses and hats to anything carried by hand.

This is the spot where Kamehameha I is believed to have forced the soldiers of the king of Oahu over the 1,000-foot cliffs in 1795 to unite the Islands. It is estimated that between 400 and 20,000 warriors jumped or were pushed over the "pali." Casualty lists were casually kept in those times. Their bones were taken by souvenir hunters from the ledges at the base of the cliffs for a hundred years afterward. Until the new road was built in the late 1950s, the site was part of the Old Pali Highway leading back and forth over the mountains. Travelers used to stop here on the old two-lane road to enjoy the panorama of the sea, shore and mountains. Thankfully, the view has not changed much despite the encroachment of the 20th century.

The light is generally considered best and the views most dependable in the mid-morning hours. If you arrive between noon and 5 p.m. you are more likely to miss the tourists.

THE OLD PALI HIGHWAY
Distance: ½ mile
Permit requirements: none
Difficulty: family

Visitors and locals alike get here from Honolulu by driving northwest seven miles on the main highway through the city (H-1), turning on the Pali Highway (Route 61), and following the signs to the Pali Lookout. There is no public transportation and it cannot be reached on foot, but tour bus rides can be arranged from most hotels.

From the small parking area, a short trail leads to the broad panorama. If you are looking for a more challenging hike in, there are two alternatives right at the lookout. You can hike back down the access road on the route toward Honolulu from the Windward Coast on the other side of the mountains. It offers about a 1½-mile trek through a lush tropical rainforest with dense evergreen trees. If this is the first island you have explored, you will be surprised by the vegetation.

Enormous philodendra grow wild, with three-foot leaves and vines climbing hundreds of feet up into the trees.

It is also possible to hike part of the way down the windward face of the mountain on the Old Pali Highway. Prudence suggests that you stick to that roadway rather than venturing over the rocks because portions are washed away from time to time by the storms that beat the summit. It is not wise to hike up into the hills as the rocks are loose and the cliffs tricky. After Diamond Head, this is where most emergency helicopter rescues take place.

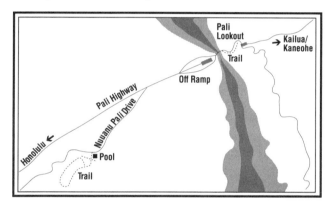

From the lookout and the short trails around it, the broad panorama of the east side starts at the bedroom community of Lanikai to the south up the coast past the magic little island known as Chinaman's Hat. The Hawaiian name is Kokolii (little dragon), and some say it is the tip of the dragon's tail you can see above the waves. In between are the twin towns of Kailua and Kaneohe, first settled as suburbs in the 1950s after the road made daily transportation feasible.

The hiking trail itself begins at the 1,186-foot Nuuanu Pali Lookout in the Kaneohe Forest Reserve. Originally a foot path, it was made a horse trail in 1845 and later widened to make room for carriages. Today, a modest highway and tunnels through the mountain speed travelers to Windward Oahu. There is a ramp to the right of the lookout that leads down part of the Old Pali Highway – or what is left of it. While there are gale force winds at the summit, there are no winds on the old road, so it is easy to enjoy the views and take pictures of the amazing panorama. The most beautiful close-up sight is of the 3,000-foot cliffs of the Koolau Mountains, harshly fluted and heavy with vegetation. They drop sharply to the broad plateau, with its vast patches of banana trees and ranch lands stretching to the sea.

It is wisest to proceed cautiously down the old road since it tends to be damp and slippery in places and falling rocks can cause hazards. There is a brook on the right a few hundred yards from the lookout, and a short walk upstream will bring you to a small stream and a great place for picnicking.

The overwhelming feeling of the mountains and the unforgettable view will remind you why these are called the Islands of Paradise. On the way back to town, there are more short trails you can take to explore the mountains.

JUDD MEMORIAL TRAIL
Distance: ½ mile
Permit requirements: none
Difficulty: family

Visitors with rented cars can turn off the Pali Highway and onto the Old Pali Highway at the first left on the way back down the mountain. From there, turn onto the Nuuanu Pali Drive for a half-mile to Reservoir No. 2 spillway just before a bridge marked 1931 (for the year it was built).

The hike to the Jackass-Ginger Pool in the Nuuanu Stream is delightful and an easy outing for a family.

The trail begins east of the spillway and downhill from the road, then reaches the Nuuanu Stream (meaning cool height) after a few hundred feet. The large rocks in the stream make a natural bridge to cross, but it should be done with caution. On the other side of the brook, the trail goes into a beautiful bamboo thicket, climbs into a eucalyptus grove, and continues into a cool stand of Norfolk Island Pines. Native to Australia's Norfolk Island, these famous evergreens were introduced to Hawaii as windbreaks and for their tough timber. The smaller trees are used a lot locally for Christmas.

The site itself was dedicated as the Charles S. Judd Memorial Grove in 1953, and the forest was named in honor of this, the first "local boy" who held the position of Territorial Forester. There are many mud-sliding chutes in the area, and when they are damp it is possible to toboggan down them using a plastic sheet, pili grass or ti leaves – a popular sport with ancient Hawaiian royalty.

The trail winds along the forest reserve boundary near a posh residential area, then turns downhill toward the Nuuanu Stream through a maze of guava and hau brush. A short way from the dense thicket, the trail passes above the Jackass-Ginger Pool.

It is easy to get back to the trailhead by retracing the route to the road. There is also a shorter route going north from the pool through the bushes a short distance to the Nuuanu Pali Drive and an easy hike back to the trailhead. And then it is back to Waikiki. This trek in the mountains shows another side of paradise few visitors ever dream exists.

5

The Koolaus

Punchbowl, the National Memorial Cemetery of the Pacific in a 112-acre extinct crater, is the last resting place for 25,000 American servicemen. It was called Puowaina (the Hill of Sacrifice) by ancient Hawaiians and was the site of prehistoric human sacrifice rituals.

From Punchbowl to Manoa Falls at the peak of a valley by the same name, the Koolau Mountains offer 10 individual hiking trails that criss-cross and zig-zag through the incredibly beautiful range and its rainforest. They feature some of the best elevated views of Honolulu, great chances for hiking, and wonderful opportunities for picnicking and fresh-water swimming.

Those familiar with Hawaii will know about Punchbowl, which dominates downtown Honolulu. It used to be possible to drive into the crater, but now you either have to hike or take a shuttle bus.

The most famous graves there for most Americans are those of World War II correspondent Ernie Pyle, and the Hawaiian astronaut who died in the 1986 Challenger disaster, Ellison Onizuko.

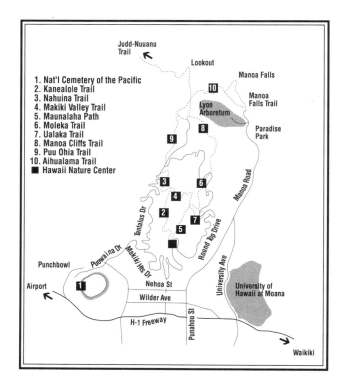

1. Nat'l Cemetery of the Pacific
2. Kanealole Trail
3. Nahuina Trail
4. Makiki Valley Trail
5. Maunalaha Path
6. Moleka Trail
7. Ualaka Trail
8. Manoa Cliffs Trail
9. Puu Ohia Trail
10. Aihualama Trail
■ Hawaii Nature Center

PUNCHBOWL
Distance: 1 mile
Permit requirements: none
Rating: family

A drive to the parking lot or a ride on city Bus No. 15 takes you to a spot near Puowaina Drive, where the scenic walk into the cemetery begins. For details, pick up a pamphlet in the Veterans Administration offices near the main flagpole.

If you hike to the lookout, you will see downtown Honolulu and the modern state capitol at your feet. In the distance to the west, you can see the giant commercial aircraft taking off from the unique reef runway at Honolulu International and the distant hills of Waianae which Robert Louis Stevenson so loved when he visited here in the last century.

For an abundant variety of other trails in the Makiki Valleys, on the Tantalus Drive, around Round Top, and up the Manoa Valley, you can head farther into the hills. There are trails to suit every hiker's ability and choosing.

Tantalus and Round Top Drives combine to make a popular car tour high above Honolulu. This is a favorite area for locals to show off the city to visiting relatives and friends. Most hikers familiar with the area like to start their hiking explorations on the Punchbowl side of the mountains and work their way gradually toward Diamond Head and Manoa Valley.

KANEALOLE HIKE
Distance: ½ mile
Permit requirements: none
Rating: family

The path to the west of the Kanealole Stream is likely to be damp and slick, but it is a gentle climb. The trail tags along an old road used by work crews to trim the vegetation in the rainforest.

The hike is all uphill, but it is heavily shaded and cool enough for the whole family. The plant life along the way is especially colorful and most visitors feel it is worth buying a local guidebook to all the unusual tropical vegetation.

NAHUINA TRAIL
Distance: 1 mile
Permit requirements: none
Rating: strenuous family

This path was built in 1979 by the Hawaii Chapter of the Sierra Club to link the Makiki Valley and Tantalus hiking areas. It creates a lot of loop hiking trails which previously had been only individual spurs.

The trail begins about 150 yards down from Tantalus Drive to the east (Diamond Head side). Unlike the Kanealole Trail, however, this one is all downhill. It can be muddy and slippery, and it is often overgrown so caution is urged. Nevertheless, the trail offers beautiful vistas of the city and Waikiki.

MAKIKI VALLEY TRAIL
Distance: 2 miles
Permit requirements: none
Rating: family

The trail begins about two miles above Makiki Heights Drive on Thntalus and descends eastward through a forest into Makiki Valley. Look for springs in the brush to the left of the intersection where it meets the Kanealole Trail.

Visitors have found the spot enchanting for a century. There is an abundance of the black and white plant called Job's Tears, which can be picked and strung into attractive jewelry.

The winding trail makes for good exercise and, if you get hungry, you can enjoy Hawaii's luscious mountain apples – another delight few visitors expect.

MAUNALAHA PATH
Distance: ½ mile
Permit requirements: none
Rating: family

The hike on this trail is an easy downhill walk from the Makiki Valley Trail. It winds around Makiki Ridge through juniper, eucalyptus, bamboo, and avocado plants. There are breaks from time to time in the rainforest that offer great views of Honolulu and Manoa Valley to the east.

Running through more beautiful vegetation, it finally crosses a foot bridge over a stream, passes through the Territorial Nursery, then returns to the base parking lot.

MOLEKA TRAIL
Distance: 1 mile
Permit requirements: none
Rating: strenuous family

This trail was also built in 1979 by Sierra Club volunteers. It is well maintained and easy to find and follow.

Descending from Round Top, it goes into a natural garden of ti, ginger, bamboo, and beautiful heliconia – a lobster-claw plant many visitors to Hawaii have never seen. The trail winds gently around the valley wall, with a lot of good views of Makiki Valley.

UALAKAA TRAIL
Distance: ½ mile
Permit requirements: none
Rating: family

This path was built in 1980 by the Sierra Club to link Puu Ualakaa State Park with the Makiki/Tantalus hiking area. From its trailhead just below the park at telephone pole #9, it climbs to Round Top Drive.

MANOA CLIFFS TRAIL
Distance: 6 miles
Permit requirements: none
Rating: strenuous family

A sign identifying the trail can be found just three miles up the Tantalus Drive. The trail is well marked and easy to follow. The first part of the trail is heavily forested and winds around the hillside. The Division of Forestry estimates there are 33 species of native plants here, many of which are identified by markers.

About a mile from the beginning of the trail, it joins the Puu Ohia Trail at Pauoa Flats, and starts zig-zagging up and down the hillside. From there to the end, the trail offers spectacular views of the valley.

PUU OHIA TRAIL
Distance: 4 miles
Permit requirements: none
Rating: strenuous family

The trailhead is easy to find, a half-mile from the Manoa Cliffs Trailhead near the top of Round Top and Tantalus Drives and not far from a parking area. The first half-mile of the path follows a winding route up the hill. Then it straightens out and goes along the side of a ridge where a number of trails head off down to the right. You can bear left and follow the trail to the point where it meets a paved road, then follow it to the end.

The Puu Ohia Trail is wide but steep, so it is important to proceed with caution until you reach Pauoa Flats. Although the trail over the flats is level, there are exposed roots and the surface is slippery so it can be a real bone-breaker.

MANOA FALLS TRAIL
Distance: ½ mile
Permit requirements: none
Rating: family

Most visitors drive to this area of the Koolaus. It is an easy trip on Manoa Road past Paradise Park and Lyon Arboretum to the end of the road. If you are on Tantalus, however, you can hike back and forth on the trails built by the Sierra Club.

Most of the Manoa Falls Trail is muddy because of heavy rains – which also account for the amazingly dense vegetation. It is well-maintained by the state and is easy to follow through the forest reserve. You can see the falls themselves from a number of points along the trail and the jungle setting makes this an enchanting place to swim and picnic.

The Division of Forestry prohibits hiking above the falls, where a number of hikers have been lost and never found. The area is highly dangerous and should be avoided.

AIHUALAMA TRAIL
Distance: 3 miles
Permit requirements: none
Rating: strenuous family

This trail begins 50 feet from the falls and follows a gentle path to Pauoa Flats. After about 150 yards, there is a great vista of upper and lower Manoa Falls, as well as another view across Manoa Valley. A little farther along, you'll be able to see Diamond Head and Waikiki. There are enough enormous banyans and beautiful ginger to excite any hiker. Then the trail begins a series of sharp switch-backs.

Just before Pauoa Flats, it cuts through a bamboo forest filled with unique sounds and sights as the winds whish through the vegetation. At the end of the trail, there are beautiful views back up into the Nuuanu Valley high in the rugged mountains they call the Koolaus.

6

Honolulu: A City On The Waterfront

Distance: 4-8 miles
Permit requirements: none
Rating: family

Honolulu is one of the few cities in the world with many of its historic buildings remaining from the first half-century of its founding, and all within walking distance of one another. Today, you can follow the development of Honolulu from a dusty village to a modern city, where the government buildings stand side-by-side with the only royal palace in America, a coral church, and New England frame houses.

Sightseeing on foot in Honolulu can be a truly fascinating experience, as Chinatown takes visitors to the mystery of the Orient just a few paces away from the original mission settlement. It is a modern city, but suffused with the beauty and languor of Polynesia.

The place to start is on the waterfront because that is where Honolulu was born. It is also the most picturesque and pleasant part of the downtown area. The town of Honolulu grew up around the sheltered harbor in the early 1800s. This refuge was first discovered by a British sea captain in the 1790s. He named it "Fair Haven." Vessels in the China Trade put into Honolulu for refreshments, repairs, and sandalwood, while whaling ships stopped here for supplies and crew. As the town grew, Kamehameha I acknowledged its importance by setting up his residence in thatched houses near the harbor. The village then became the center of activity for the monarchy.

Honolulu is joining the growing number of American maritime centers that are redeveloping their waterfronts. The crowning jewel of Honolulu Harbor's rebirth is the Aloha Tower Marketplace, a family gathering place modeled after Baltimore's Inner Harbor and Boston's Quincy Market. With ample parking nearby, it is the best place to start a walk around town. Its setting on the shores of the historic, bustling Honolulu Harbor distinguishes it from purely recreational waterfront developments, which tend to be too far removed from working harbors to do more than simulate activity. In contrast, the marketplace offers you the chance to see, hear, and feel a busy port going about its everyday business as you learn about the history of Hawaii in a retail and dining environment.

The next stop is the 10th-floor observation deck of the Aloha Tower, where the harbor and city meet. There are photographs and displays of old Honolulu Harbor and the 360-degree view lets you see how the whole city is laid out. The older city is tucked among the vast glass towers, a quaint and fascinating place waiting to be discovered.

The brownstone Dillingham Transportation Building between Queen and Nimitz Streets is a classic remnant of the 1930s. Diagonally across the street standing like

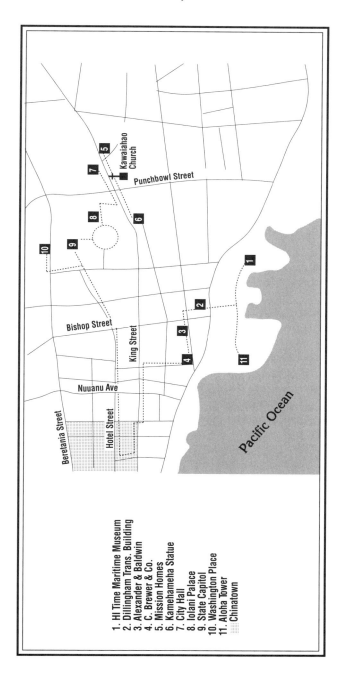

Kawaiahao Church
Punchbowl Street
Bishop Street
King Street
Nuuanu Ave
Beretania Street
Hotel Street
Pacific Ocean

1. HI Time Maritime Museum
2. Dillingham Trans. Building
3. Alexander & Baldwin
4. C. Brewer & Co.
5. Mission Homes
6. Kamehameha Statue
7. City Hall
8. Iolani Palace
9. State Capitol
10. Washington Place
11. Aloha Tower
    Chinatown

a matching book end is the Alexander & Baldwin Building from the same era, but with different ornamentation.

The surrounding towers represent the remains from yesteryear of Amfac Inc., Theo H. Davies & Co. Ltd. and Castle & Cooke Inc., three of the "Big Five" corporations which dominated Honolulu when sugar was king. The most venerable of all "Big Five" firms, however, was C. Brewer & Co., Ltd. Its two-storey building was dedicated in 1930 and today is nestled in a tropical garden surrounded by a stone wall just one block toward the airport on Queen Street – as picturesque as it was the day it opened.

Up toward the hills, you will find Honolulu's Chinatown, said to be more Asian than even those of San Francisco and Seattle. It combines the old with the new, historic preservation with design innovation. Here you can seek out Fook Sauy Tong, a Chinese herb specialist, and Suen Hang Yee, an acupuncturist, a Chinese cake shop, and the famed Hop Hing Market. Back in the 1840s the first issue of *The Polynesian* carried an ad by Sam & Low, bakers from Canton. About 1886, a Chinese baker named Wo Fat went into business on Hotel Street. Today, the remnants of Wo Fat's chop suey house set the tone for the architecture of Chinatown.

A hike down the newly renovated and restored Hotel Street, limited to pedestrian and bus traffic, will transport you back to the reality of the 20th century and the modern, recently restored State Capitol building completed in 1969. One of the newest in the nation, it is set in a reflecting pond symbolizing the state's relationship with the sea. The cone-shaped legislative chambers symbolize Hawaiian volcanoes, and the 40 flared pillars its royal palms. Replicas of the State Seal, each 15 feet in diameter and weighing 7,500 pounds, are suspended over the two entrances. The spacious central court is open to the skies and expresses Hawaii's indoor-outdoor mode of living. A statue of Father Damien at the entrance facing the mountains and another of Queen Liliuokalani facing the Iolani Palace are a tribute to Hawaii's attachment to its rich and sometimes tragic history.

Toward the sea and through the deep shade of an immense banyan stands the Iolani Palace, built by King David Kalakaua in 1882 and his official residence until he died in 1891. His sister-successor, Queen Liliuokalani, occupied it until the overthrow of the monarchy in 1893. From then until 1968, it was used as the capital of the Republic, then the Territory, and finally the State of Hawaii – although visitors are more likely to remember the building from its starring days as headquarters for McGarrett in *Hawaii Five-0.*

Today, it has been entirely restored to its original grandeur by the Friends of the Iolani Palace, with many of the rooms furnished in period. None is finer, however, than the magnificent throne room, with a suffused pink glow which the last King adored. It is open to the public, but you are advised to make reservations.

Next door is the Hawaii State Library, partially funded by Andrew Carnegie and designed by his brother-in-law, Henry D. Whitfield. Completed in 1913, it has a large central garden court which makes a quiet spot to read and relax.

One more block toward Diamond Head you will find Honolulu Hale (City Hall), a mixture of styles but mostly Spanish. It was completed in 1927 and, like most other historic buildings here, it reflects the outdoor lifestyle and design trends in Hawaii of the early 20th century. It is completely unlike any other city hall in the United States.

Across the street, the Mission Houses Museum is a rare find. The Mission Houses were dedicated as a

National Historic Landmark in 1965 and are operated as an historic house museum under the auspices of the Hawaiian Children's Society. Seven couples, five children, and three Hawaiian youths who had been educated in Connecticut made up the Pioneer Company of missionaries sent from Boston in 1819. Eleven companies of reinforcements followed through 1848. In June, 1820, the New England missionaries were granted land on which to settle, about a half-mile from the village of Honolulu on the road to Waikiki. On this site are the Frame House (1821), the Chamberlain Depository (1831), and the Printing House (1841). Next door stands the Kawaiahao Church. Four grass houses of worship, each larger than the one before, preceded the present day church built from 14,000 blocks of coral in 1842.

A little farther back toward downtown is a gold statue of King Kamehameha I, a duplicate of which stands in Statuary Hall in the U.S. Capital. This statue of the chief who unified the warring islands of Hawaii into one kingdom was erected to commemorate the centennial of Captain James Cook's discovery of Hawaii. Aliiolani Hale provides the backdrop to the statue. Kalakaua officially opened it at the beginning of the 1874 legislative session, and it housed the legislature, cabinet offices, and courts during the reigns of Kalakaua and Liliokalani.

On the mountain side of the street from the State Capitol stands Washington Place, another National Historic Site. Built by an American sea captain for his family in 1846, today this is the official residence of the Governor of Hawaii and is not open to the public.

Next door and under the slopes of Punchbowl is St. Andrew's Cathedral, built in 1867. Queen Victoria of England, to whom the Hawaiian royal family felt an affinity, granted a license for the establishment of an Anglican missionary bishop in Hawaii at the request of King Kamehameha IV and Queen Emma, and the church and its priory were very much the work of the royal family of Hawaii.

Our Lady of Peace Cathedral can be found at the top of downtown on the way to the new State Capitol. From its grounds, there is an unobstructed view down Bishop Street to the harbor.

On the way back to Waikiki, whether on foot or in a car, you will pass Ala Moana Center shopping complex. It is on 50 acres just west of Waikiki. More than 42 million visitors stop here every year, triple the visitor count at Disneyland.

Across the main street into Waikiki is Ala Moana Beach, a favorite hangout for local residents. It offers over a mile of reef close to the shore.

Hikers making the long walk back should make sure to take plenty of water with them. The fair breezes make the weather seem moderate most of the year, but the tropical sun is punishing and you may become dehydrated and even faint if you don't have enough liquids.

7

Nature On The
North Shore

WAIMEA ARBORETUM AND
BOTANICAL GARDEN TRAIL
Distance: 1½ miles, 4 miles of spurs
Permit requirements: none
Rating: family

Waimea Falls Park is located on the North Shore of
Oahu overlooking one of Hawaii's most famous
surfing beaches, just a few miles north of the quaint
seaside town of Haleiwa. In ancient times, this was the
most sacred site on the island.

A marked turn-off leads inland from Highway 83,
which circles the island's Windward Coast. It leads to
the park, where there is a small charge for admission.
Circle Island Bus 52 also goes past the turn-off to the
park.

The garden along the main trail is very special to
Hawaii. It is the Waimea Arboretum and Botanical

Garden. With a sister on Kauai, its goal is to cultivate as many surviving species of plants native to Hawaii as possible. No American garden faces a more daunting task because the native flora of Hawaii is by far the most critically endangered in the United States. Of 1,800 native plants, more than 800 are federally listed as threatened or endangered, according to Kieth Woolliams, director of the garden. Woolliams says it is important to understand that this special island chain is the most remote archipelago in the world – 2,300 miles from the American mainland and 4,000 miles from Japan – and the plant life that has evolved in Hawaii is like nothing else on earth.

A beautiful hiking trail begins just over a bridge crossing Waimea Stream. One branch leads downstream a short way to palm and hibiscus collections. The main trail leads up the valley on a hillside through an extensive botanical collection. It also passes through rebuilt ancient Hawaiian living sites and native stonework. Eventually, the trail crosses Kaiwikoele Stream and climbs around the nose of a ridge, leaving the garden area, and goes slowly uphill above Waimea Stream, where it ends.

It is a good idea to return through the gardens, leaving plenty of time to see the tremendous collections. A swim in the pool at the stream headwaters can be refreshing before starting the hike back. The rich variety of branching trails is better to explored on the way back, before losing track of time.

"Hawaii was really an open book for all that plant life," according to Woolliams. "There were no grazing animals, no need for plants to develop spines, no need for poisons ... and no man. Hawaii was unoccupied so plants could move into the open spaces with no competition. But native flora began to disappear with the arrival of Polynesian man with and slash and burn mathods. Most of the low vegetation was gone by the time Captain Cook arrived and, today, half the surviving species are endangered. Waimea is serious about its conservation program; for example, it has erythrinas that are critically endangered, but which have more alkaloids than any other plants ever studied," Woolliams explains. "The potential medical and economic consequences are so profound they cannot even be estimated."

Because of Waimea Valley's low elevation and rocky terrain, many species thrive there. "We are big on plants at Waimea, but we're short on facilities," says Woolliams.

Beginning with an 1,800-acre unplanted landscape in 1974, the arboretum has carefully plotted, planted and organized over 30 gardens along the four miles of hiking trails. Beneath ancient trees and alongside historic stone formations, the staff has paid homage to the past by creating a living and permanent array of tropical plants. Any visit provides memories to last a lifetime. There is something awesome about seeing a healthy plant and realizing that it is the last one of its kind on earth.

Two of the most exotic and special gardens in the valley are the ginger and heliconia collections, both the largest collections of their kind in the world. A hike through their rugged terrain is a great introduction to the lush vegetation of Hawaii. In the same area, heliconia grow up to 20 feet tall and produce the brilliantly colorful bracts that are familiar to kama'ainas (islanders).

The hibiscus evolutionary garden stands at the base of the hiking trail and is the only one of its kind in the world. It traces the evolution of the spectacular hibiscus flowers that are the symbol and state flower of Hawaii.

Archeological excavation and investigation is also a full-time activity at Waimea. Several historical sites have been uncovered by the staff, which includes one of the few prehistorians in Hawaii.

The lush meadows and cool, shady trees at Waimea are a haven for many native and introduced species of birds and wildlife. A variety of native birds such as the white-tailed tropicbird and the Hawaiian owl, as well as introduced species such as the common Indian mynah bird and the red-crested cardinal, make the park their home. The beautiful peacocks were a favorite with Hawaiian royalty, and retire high into the monkeypod trees every night. Each morning, they swoop down for another day of preening and primping at Waimea.

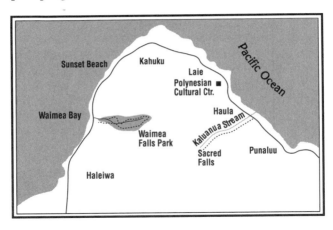

SACRED FALLS TRAIL
Distance: 4½ miles
Permit requirements: none
Rating: strenuous family

There is another valley a few miles south of Waimea that ancient Hawaiians also believed was sacred. It is a great hike through nature but, unlike Waimea, it can be dangerous so caution is advised. The waterfalls are fed by streams high in the Koolau Mountains, making flash floods possible even when the weather around the trail is fair and dry. Hikers have been killed, so posted warnings must be heeded.

Legends have it that the pool at the base of the falls is bottomless, leading to another world where a demon lives. It is a great place for picnicking and the trail offers lots of fruit for picking along the way.

From the trailhead, it is 1¼ mile on a cane road to the valley trail. Ahead, hikers can see the narrow canyon that surrounds the falls. The trail begins at a flat grassy area that once was a parking lot. On the left side of this large, open area, the road turns into a trail which crosses a dry stream bed and gently climbs up into the canyon. Before long it reaches the Kaluanua Stream, which is easy to wade across, or you can hop on the rocks to keep your feet dry. Past the stream are countless mountain apple trees, bearing delicious little red apples in season. The bountiful area is said to be the home of Kamapuaa (child of a pig) who was half-human and half-hog. Near the end of the valley, there is a dry falls which is the site, according to the legends, where Kamapuaa turned himself into a giant boar so that his followers could escape a charging army by climbing up his back for safety to the ledge far above the trail.

Sacred Falls itself can be heard crashing to the valley floor and can be seen around the next turn in the hiking path (after another stream crossing). The valley walls are 1,600 feet, but the falls themselves only drop 90 feet. There is a beautiful pool at the base, but it is usually muddy and a bit chilly for swimming. In addition, unseen rocks make fresh water swimming a questionable undertaking. But it is fun to splash in the stream just below the pool and to picnic in the cool shade on the large rocks.

LAIE

Distance: 6 miles
Permit requirements: none
Rating: strenuous

Laie, a small town just south of Sacred Falls, attracts thousands of tourists – not for hiking to its beautiful valley, but to visit the Polynesian Cultural Center. It is owned and operated by the Mormon Church of Hawaii, which was founded there almost a century ago.

From the gate at the end of Poohaili Road, a hiking trail leads through lush fruit trees up along Kahawaimui Stream, where climbers can enjoy a little pool with waterfalls.

The main trail continues along the ridge and is well defined most of the way. When the weather is clear, there is a panorama all the way from Mokuleia, where professional glider pilots take visitors skyward for breathtaking views, to the Waianae Mountain range sheltering the Leeward Coast of Oahu. Continuing up the road goes near Kaena, which truly seems like the end of the world. It used to be possible to drive around the point, at least by four-wheel-drive vehicle, but a 1988 storm washed out the last of the road.

8

Outings On Leeward Oahu

Many regret the ruin of what was once a pristine paradise, but that is mainly true for the visitors who refuse to leave the confines of a few developed resort areas and the comfort of their rented cars.

For hikers in search of special treks, there are limitless opportunities. The most popular trails offer spectacular views.

There are other more remote destinations that you may have to go out of your way to find. Some of the best are on the Leeward Coast, which has no tourist meccas at all.

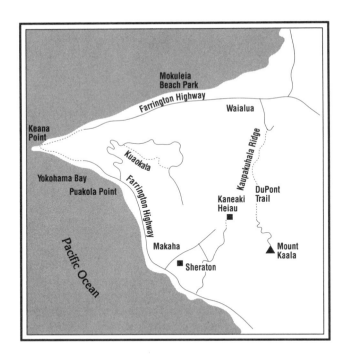

DUPONT TRAIL
Distance: 8 miles
Permit requirements: Division of Forestry,
Waialua Sugar Company, and Waialua
Ranch Partners with 24-hour advance notice
Rating: difficult

Mt. Kaala – easy to identify by the white-domed radar installations at its peak – is the highest point on Oahu and the climb is the most difficult on the island. The last mile of the trail is dangerous and requires the skills of experienced hikers. Sections of the trail traverse narrow ledges along 2,000-foot cliffs plunging to the valley floor below. Ropes have been installed to help hikers in the most precarious places, but this is still a trip only for the stout of heart.

The trail starts at the Forest Reserve boundary 1½ miles beyond the second gate on the jeep road out of Waialua. A wealth of native plants, not found anywhere else on earth, can be found in the forest. Many of them are not only indigenous, but very critically endangered.

The trail is uneven and the footing can be loose, but the views of the island's north side and of the deep gouges in the mountains make it well worth the climb. The last mile is a sheer climb up 1,800 feet. It is important to test the ropes before depending on them.

The cliffs then come to an end and a paved road leads you to the summit a quarter-mile away. Military officials do not welcome visitors, but the 4,000-foot-high, mile-wide plateau that is the summit of Mt. Kaala offers views of the island which can only be described as sublime.

It is a rough climb back down the steep trail. Alternatively, you can opt to follow the 8½-mile roadwith the hope of catching a ride with one of the service vehicles.

KAENA POINT
Distance: 4 miles
Permit requirements: none
Rating: strenuous family

At the end of the road out to Leeward Oahu is Kaena Point, a remote spot whose desolation has an overwhelming quality all of its own. Like the far tip of the Algarve in Portugal, this place seems like the end of the world.

It has always been difficult to drive around this distant tip of Oahu, even by four-wheel vehicle. But a New Year's storm in 1988 washed out the last of the unpaved road and now the only way to see this unique spot is on foot – an experience not to be missed if you have a sense of adventure.

It is possible to approach from either direction. You can start out from the foot of Mt. Kaala at Waialua on the Leeward Coast or fromMokuleia if you are visiting the North Shore. The cool northerly tradewinds and sea offer welcome relief along this hot and dusty hike. It is possible to follow most of the old roads or walk along the shore.

Whichever you choose, you will discover a magic isolation in this area which you would never expect after an evening in Waikiki.

KANEAKI HEIAU
Distance: 1 mile
Permit requirements: none
(open 10 a.m. to 2 p.m. daily)
Rating: family

If you are already hiking the Leeward Coast you will find it worth your time to trek up to this little-visited spot. Drive out the coast road to Makaha and take the turn to the Sheraton resort overlooking the deep blue Pacific. At the top of the hill, you can follow the road out of the parking lot about 50 feet to a path which leads directly to a heiau (ancient temple). Restored in 1970, Kaneaki is one of the best preserved "precontact" places of worship on Oahu. Built in the 13th century, it was first used as a temple to agricultural gods, then became a temple to the war gods. Interpretive signs identify a number of ceremonial sites and structures which have been rebuilt.

A stroll through the historic site gives visitors a feeling of the important role such religious and cultural sites played in prehistoric Hawaii. Reconstructions include a priest house, a drum house, an altar, a number of kikis (images), and two anuus (towers of worship). The lush vegetation of the area enhances the natural beauty of both the heiau and of Makaha Valley. Guava and papaya are readily available and ripe for picking. Red and white hibiscus (the state flower) and striking heliconia plants create a rainbow of natural colors high above the valley floor. And the wonderful kukui trees and tropical breezes keep the area comfortable, if not always cool.

KUAOKALA TRAIL
Distance: 4½-mile circle trail
Permit requirements: Division of Forestry
Rating: strenuous

The access road to the Kuaokala Road is in a military district, so permission is an absolute requirement. The magnificent views and moving solitude make it a hike well worth taking.

The trailhead can be found in the small parking area. The route starts out descending a paved path and continues on a dirt road almost three miles. This initial part of the trail is lined with beautiful guava trees, and their fruit is wonderful when it is in season. After about a mile of hiking up and down small turns through eucalyptus and cypress trees, the trail reaches a ridge with magnificent panoramas of the rarely-seen saddle between the two great mountain ranges of Oahu and the lush valleys of Leeward Oahu.

After a sharp downhill stretch, the trail climbs to an 1,800-foot perch with breathtaking views of the Makua Valley and the West Coast of Oahu. The spurs off to both sides offer more great views and some wonderful spots for picnicking.

It is a long drive back into Honolulu, but one of the most beautiful in Hawaii. The stretch down the Leeward Coast offers many panoramic views of the sea and its crashing waves. This coast has no protective reef, unlike most of Hawaii's shorelines.

At Kahe Point, the southern end of the Leeward Coast, lies Ko Olina, Oahu's only new world-class resort, and Ihilani Resort & Spa, its first and – so far – only hotel. Ko Olina also features Oahu's newest golf course, which is already a favorite with aficianados. After the turn eastward at Barber's Point, the road offers a number of good views of Diamond Head and downtown Honolulu sitting under the dramatic Koolau Mountains. The seldom-used Leeward beaches along the way are so beautiful that they were used in filming the movie *Hawaii*.

If you have the time, you may want to stop at the Arizona Memorial in Pearl Harbor. It has a "touristy" reputation with many mainlanders, but it is one of the most moving spots in America.

December 7, 1941 is still a "day which will live in infamy" but today, in stark contrast to the mayhem that descended on the harbor that early morning long ago, Pearl Harbor is calm and tranquil. No one visiting the Memorial, however, can fail to be moved by the sad memories and profound sense of loss it evokes. The shoreline waiting arrangements have been vastly improved in recent years. The modern Visitors Center includes boat docks and an attractive building with a museum, a movie theatre, a bookstore and a snack bar.

A launch takes visitors directly to the Memorial, a 184-foot floating bridge of white concrete dedicated in 1961. It spans the width of the sunken *U.S.S. Arizona*, which stands upright on the bottom in 38 feet of water. There is a flag mounted on one of the few parts of the ship's superstructure still breaking the placid surface of the water.

The Arizona Memorial is Hawaii's most popular visitor attraction, and no one coming here should miss the profound experience. It helps provide the memories that make a vacation in Hawaii an experience of a lifetime.

Maui

9

Haleakala

Distance: 30 miles
Permit requirements: Haleakala National Park
Rating: strenuous

On a clear day, you can see Maui easily from the South Coast of Oahu. The beautiful "Valley Island" is the second largest of the islands in Hawaii and ranks number two in terms of visitors.

Haleakala, the massive mountain that is East Maui, is the largest dormant volcano in the world. Its hardened lava rises 30,000 feet up off the sea floor. At its peak, up a winding road 10,000 feet above sea level, is Haleakala Crater. This is the one spot you really must visit on Maui, called the House of the Sun, and the best way to discover it is to hike into the crater itslef.

The National Park Service maintains 30 miles of well-marked trails and three cabins costing just $4 a night – but they have to be booked months in advance. This marvel of nature is so enormous that all of Manhattan could fit within its rim, and the tallest skyscraper would only be as tall as one of the cones on its floor.

From the summit, a stunning panorama of lunar-like desolation fills the horizon. The best time to see it is at dawn when the sun keeps its daily appointment with Pele, the volcano goddess, and paints the volcanic landscape with a kaleidoscope of colors. A century ago Mark Twain called this "the sublimest spectacle I ever witnessed. There is truly nothing else like it in all the world."

There are two principal trails through the crater: Sliding Sands/Halemauu Trail, which runs north and south; and Sliding Sands/Kaupo Gap Trail, which runs east and west. The two have the distinct advantages over others that they pass by all three cabins. And, of course, it is possible to climb them both in connection with many of the side trails in the crater.

Haleakala's trails traverse ground that can be covered with snow in winter, and they can be cold and wet just about anytime. The air is thin at this elevation and the vegetation is sparse. Running water is only available at the three strategically placed cabins.

The magnificent silversword plants that can be found nowhere else on earth are wonders to behold. In the time of Mark Twain, they were so plentiful that native Hawaiians threw them down into the mighty crater in an ancient game of bowling. Almost extinct after World War II, they are enjoying a rebirth thanks to the conservation efforts of the National Park Service.

Hikers going into the crater have to get permits at the park headquarters. This takes less than three days unless the plan includes using the cabins or one of the campsites (in which case it can take a month and applications should be made in writing three months in advance).

There are several good points along the 10-mile road between park headquarters and the peak where you can stretch your legs with short hikes to appreciate the magnificent views. At 8,000 feet above sea level, you can take a one-mile walk on Halemauu Trail to the rim of the crater, with a great view across Koolau Gap, down Keanae Valley, and across the zig-zagging trail down the sheer wall of the crater. There is another remarkable view at 8,800 feet from the Leleiwi Overlook, about 350 yards from the rugged road. Here, in the late afternoons, you can catch a unique view of your silhouette on the rainbows created by the misty, high-elevation showers.

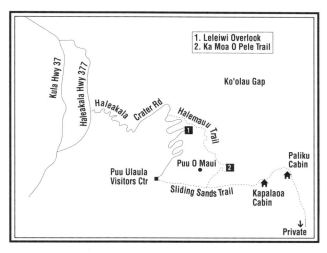

A little higher up, stop at the Kalahaku Overlook where there are exhibits explaining the crater's cones and lava flow along with some of the famous silversword plants. The plants flower only once in 20 years and then die, but their seeds start the process of creation anew, much like the volcanoes that are, even today, recreating the islands of Hawaii. The silversword plants here, relatives of sun flowers, are unique, but they have some other rare relatives in the West Maui hills and on the distant Big Island of Hawaii. This is also the first spot to catch a glimpse of Mauna Kea, the giant volcano on neighboring Hawaii, as it stretches above the clouds.

From the summit of the crater road, hikers can look down on the slopes of cinder blown by the tradewinds against the rocks of the original summit. The Koolau Gap to the north and Kaupo Gap to the south cut the rim in half. And beyond Koolau, Hanakauhi's peak often protrudes through a thick blanket of clouds. Opposite, another peak sticks out like a medieval fortress against Kaupo Gap. The symmetrical cones on the floor of the vast crater look like little castles of sand, but each is, in fact, several hundred feet tall.

Puu o Maui, rising 615 feet from the floor of the crater, is the tallest. In dramatic contrast to the lunar-like landscape, the lush green vegetation of east Maui can be seen through the cracks in the crater wall, 10,000 feet farther below where the sea stretches as far as the eye can see.

A trail climbs nearly 400 feet above the visitor center past the ruins of stone barriers built by the ancients for protection against the wind. The hills are formed by a rock called andesite, which is lighter in weight and color than most of the lava in Hawaii. Walk the short distance down Sliding Sands Trail to get the feel of it. The trail is thrilling for even the most timid of visitors. But remember that the air is thin and hiking back up the slopes can be difficult.

From the Puu Ulaula Visitor Center at the peak, you get a breathtaking 360-degree panorama of the crater. On a clear day, you can see West Maui and the islands of Molokai, Oahu, Lanai, and the Big Island of Hawaii. It is easy to hike a mile past the park along Skyline Drive and through "Science City" – a satellite communications installation. Although it is not open to the public, you'll get a great view down to the South Coast desert over the Lualailua Hills.

The likes of Mark Twain have tried but failed to describe the wonders of Haleakala. The expanse of lava flows and cones gives you the feeling you may have landed on the surface of the moon at the peak of a lush tropical paradise. To see the reality of Haleakala that has stunned visitors for centuries, you have to climb or take horseback rides down into the floor of the giant crater. The two main trails, Sliding Sands and Halemauu, lead both down into and across this giant wonder of nature. They intersect at the east end of the valley near the Paliku Cabin.

Sliding Sands trail leads about six miles down the south face of the crater wall to the Kapalaoa Cabin and then northeast four miles to the Paliku Cabin. The Halemauu Trail takes you four miles down the west wall to the Holua Cabin, and then another six miles along the center of the sloping wall of the sleeping giant. A variety of spur trails connect the two at different points. It is easy to complete the round-trip hike over the Halemauu Trail to the Holua Cabin. Hikers looking for a long day's hike often prefer descending Sliding Sands, although it is advisable that you avoid this route as a way out of Haleakala because it is steep and the air is thin. Hikers should climb down Sliding Sands, cross the floor on the well-marked Ka Moa O Pele Trail, and climb out on the Halemauu Trail. It is wisest to take along a non-hiker to move the car, or to take two cars with one parked at the lower end of the trail by the exit from the canyon.

If you have no car problems and are looking for a good overnight hike, take the Halemauu Trail to the Kapalaoa Cabin one day and return the next. It is only eight miles each way, but the hiking is strenuous and there will be frequent pauses to admire the scenery.

It is important to carry your own water because the cabins are far apart and have only limited supply. Also, take a light raincoat, a jacket or sweater, and plenty of sunscreen. Make sure you are in good physical condition and have comfortable walking shoes or boots.

At rainy Paliku, the tall grasses, large native tree species, and giant ferns create a lush haven in the barren wasteland. North of Kapalaoa Cabin, there is a unique cave created when molten lava was pushed up by hot gases that later cooled in a weird geological formation.

The eerie world of the crater's interior offers a special show of sandalwood trees, Hawaiian Snow (the first plants to appear after a lava flow in the upper altitudes), the unique mountain pili (grass), and a geological tapestry, especially at sunrise, that is unforgettable.

On the Halemauu Trail, you pass a "bottomless pit," an ancient "spatter vent" which looks like a 10-foot-wide well. Nearby is Pele's Paint Pot, which you will see as you pass between cinder cones on a spur trail called Pele's Pig Pen. The lava rock here, called a'a', emerged partially solidified and filled with gases. As it cooled, it broke apart to form "clinkers," creating a tapestry of colors as the sunlight plays across them from different angles during the day.

Reservations to use the cabins must be made by mail at least 90 days in advance and are limited to three nights a month, with only two consecutive nights in a single cabin. Write to Haleakala National Park, PO Box 369, Makawao, Maui, HI 96768.

10

Lahaina

Distance: 4 miles
Permit requirements: none
Rating: family

Lahaina is still the center of the action of Maui, but the narrow dusty streets Herman Melville walked are now brightly lined with art galleries, shops, restaurants and night spots. This is also one of the best places to watch Hawaii's biggest visitors, the humpback whales, as they sing and cavort in the Molokai Channel – although the best way to see the whales is to take a boat ride out and join them at sea.

Today, the once ribald capital of the Sandwich Islands has been turned into a living museum, and you can spend hours hiking through a century and a half of Hawaiian history. Lahaina has only a narrow strip of beach and no luxury hotels, but it has memories enough to last a lifetime. In 1964, the town as a whole was made a National Historical Landmark, and it has been called the "Williamsburg of the Pacific." It is not being rebuilt as a period piece, but combines the old and the new with a charm hard to find anywhere else.

Shaw Street

Wainee Church

Lahaina Sports Park

Prison Street

7

6

Wainee Street

Luakini Street

Front Street

Banyan Tree

4

3

5

Dickenson Street

Highway 30

Lahainalua Street

The Carthaginian

Pacific Ocean

1. Masters Reading Room
2. Baldwin house
3. Courthouse
4. Fort
5. Pioneer Inn
6. Hale Paahao
7. David Malo House

Lahaina offers a self-guiding walking tour. It is easy to follow, but you should be sure to drink plenty of water, whether you carry your own or not. These are still the tropics and the sun is always strong despite the apparently benign climate.

The first stop is the Masters Reading Room, located on the corner of Front and Dickerson Streets. This shaded and peaceful home has been restored to look exactly as it did when built by missionary and physician Rev. Dwight Baldwin, who came from Durham, Connecticut in 1847. It now serves as the headquarters for the Lahaina Restoration Foundation.

The whaling years lasted through the 1860s in Lahaina, and the Reading Room provided a home for officers wishing to spend some time ashore with their families. They could watch ships at anchor, passing boats, and general activity in the village, much as visitors do today.

In the 1850s, Rev. Baldwin built the Baldwin House next door for his growing family. The home, with its furniture, equipment, aged photographs, artifacts, displays and library, gives a vivid picture of what life was like in the bustling Sandwich Islands, especially for a physician who was also a community leader. By the turn of the century, Lahaina had become a quiet plantation town, with few visitors and scarce accommodations – a situation which was not to last long. George Freeman, a dedicated Canadian mounted policeman, followed a criminal to Lahaina, fell in love with the town, and built the Pioneer Inn in 1901, which his family continued to operate until it closed 90 years later. Located across Front Street from the missionary homes, the restored inn saw few guests in those early days, so Freeman built a movie house and service station to attract attention. Today, it is a special place for visitors and residents. Stay in its rooms or enjoy the often rowdy local crowd in its bar.

By the pier in the little harbor in front of the inn is the *Carthaginian,* a replica of a 19th-century brig, typical of the small freighters that brought the first commerce to the Sandwich Islands. It is exactly the same size as the *Thaddeus,* which was famous for bringing the first company of missionaries from Boston on their 160-day sail to Hawaii.

To the south of the Pioneer Inn is another historical site simply called the Banyan Tree. Brought as a little tree from India in 1873, the giant has grown to cover an entire city block. Only eight feet tall when it was planted, today it rises more than 50 feet and covers a 200-foot area. It is a popular place for local events such as political rallies, but it's also a great spot to picnic in the cool shade and enjoy the balmy trade wind breezes.

The 19th-century courthouse still stands on the seaward side of the great tree. Built in 1859, it was the site of the customs house, post office, tax collector's office, island governor's office, police court, courtroom, and jury room.

The Fort on the Canal is little more than a pile of rocks, but it is historically significant. During the reign of King Kamehameha III, the missionary influence was wielded on visiting whaleships. Incensed whalers fired cannons at the missionary compound when a law was passed forbidding native women from swimming out to the ships to greet seamen. As a result, Governor Hoapili was given a royal command to build a fort on the waterfront in 1831.

Built in the late 1830s, the palace of King Kamehameha was known as Hale Piula (house with a tin roof) and stood at the opposite end of the little harborfront. In 1858, it was one of many buildings in Lahaina levelled by a destructive storm, and the present-day courthouse was built with material from the wreckage. Only the ruins of the palace remain today.

The unusual sometimes seems commonplace in Lahaina. Wainee Church, for example, has a history quite different from any other historic site in Lahaina. It was immortalized in James Michener's *Hawaii* as the church that just would not stand, and through its history, it has been ravaged by storms, wind, and fire. But it has been rebuilt and rebuilt again. The newest church was dedicated in 1953 and renamed Waiola (the water of life). Its front door faces mighty Kauaula Valley while the back faces the sea, so the legendary winds that have destroyed it through the years will not harm it again.

On the corner of Wainee and Prison Streets is one of the most completely preserved buildings in Lahaina, known as "The Prison." Hale Paahao (house stuck in irons) was built in the 1850s to house unruly seamen. The original fort site had been used to hold sailors overnight if they ignored warnings to return to their ships at sunset and it had a well-deserved reputation for being a rough place to spend the night. In time, the rulers of Hawaii decided to build a larger compound using convict labor and the government stripped the fort of its coral block stone to complete the construction. The scene of many happier occasions today, The Prison is frequently rented out for community events and its interior is a pleasant park-like setting every day of the year.

Visitors seeking more exercise than walking often turn to the area known today as Lahaina's sports park, but it is also the site of one of the most interesting stories about old Lahaina. There was once a large pond at this end of town called Kihawahine, home of the most powerful water spirit on Maui. Ancient Hawaiians were a people of many myths, superstitions, and gods. Dragons were ancient ghost-gods in the religion of old Hawaii, and Kihawahine was worshipped by the royal family as a special guardian. When Kamehameha I conquered Maui, he claimed this most sacred spot as his own – and it still brings good luck to the competitively-minded today.

Lahaina is no newcomer to this interest in history. Hawaii's first historical society was formed in 1836 by Kamehameha III, along with Revs. Sheldon Dibble and William Richards. They set about the business of collecting and preserving the history of the islands. David Malo was one of their principal students, and he contributed to the tradition with the first book written in the Hawaiian language. His home still stands on the edge of the historic district.

Adjacent to the missionary compound there is a small white building known as the Spring House. During the whaling era, in the mid-19th century, Lahaina was a bustling harbor serving 400 whaling ships lying at anchor to take on provisions. No commodity was more critical than fresh water. The process of getting the water to the ships in quantity was difficult and complex. The need was so obvious and taken for granted, however, that no mention of the Spring House (from which the water came) is made in the historical records of the time.

Maui's biggest visitors, the 40-ton humpback whales, are one of the unforgettable sights (and sounds) of a visit to Hawaii. Seeing them up close is an overwhelming experience, and there is no better place to do it than in Lahaina. Two-thirds of the North Pacific humpbacks winter in Hawaii to flee the cold north. The 600 to 700 whales have no enemies in Hawaii, so they play and breed freely within easy view of many land-based lookouts.

The winter whale-watching season is regarded as a prime visitor attraction. Commercial whale-watching boat cruises and helicopter flights now compete to accommodate the huge demand to see these glorious mammals.

The 50-foot singers, easily identified by long pectorals and fine white markings on their tail flukes, sing haunting songs after they migrate from the Bering Sea to find mates and give birth to calves conceived the year before. On Maui, adults are easy to see breaching, tails slapping the water and flippers flopping. Lahaina is most popular for whale watching because it is easy to arrange rides out into the Molokai Channel, where they are most numerous. One of the best perches, according to admirers, however, is a small cliff on the road to Lahaina overlooking Maalaea Bay, where so many whales are born every year that it has been dubbed the "humpback nursery."

11

The Seven Pools Of Kipahulu

Distance: 10 miles
Permit requirements: Haleakala National Park
(for camping only)
Rating: strenuous family

The way to find Maui at its beautiful, unspoiled best is to drive down the twisting road to "heavenly Hana" where the likes of George Harrison, Kris Kristofferson, and Jim Nabors have settled, and where you will experience some of the most incredible mountainside hiking in the Pacific. Here are perhaps the most spectacular seaside cliffs in Hawaii, weaving along the coast, dipping down through green-ferned valleys, and crossing ravines with waterfalls plunging to the lava-formed coast far below.

If you plan ahead, you can book one of the dozen cabins at the Waianapanapa State Park just outside Hana. They rent for only $10 per night. Nearby, idyllic Hamoa Beach has been described as "one of the most beautiful curves of sand in the world" by James Michener.

No visit to Maui is complete without paying homage to the Seven Pools where Charles Lindbergh lived and is buried. Thousands of feet of waterfalls are stretched up and down the back side of Haleakala between the enormous ponds. This is real adventure territory, leaving civilization far behind. The road deteriorates past Hana, twisting and turning over potholes, and the clearest sign warns "Caution: Pig Crossing."

About seven miles beyond Hana, Wailua and Kanahualui Falls rumble over steep lava cliffs, filling the air with a watery mist and splashing into the pools below. This is where the enormous Kipahulu Valley runs into the sea.

Palikea Stream starts far up on the southwestern side of Haleakala and steps its way down the pools until it reaches the vast Pacific. Modern visitors name these the Seven Sacred Pools, but the area is neither sacred nor are there seven pools (it's more like two dozen).

Before starting up or down the mountain on a climb, try to talk with one of the two rangers who can usually be found in or near the parking area. They know a great deal about the natural history of the area and can warn visitors of the few dangers they should watch for, such as the flash floods that can come up fast in the pools.

It is important for hikers to bring their own water; there is no drinkable water available in the area. It is sometimes crowded in the parking lot, but seldom along the trail. This is, in part, because most residents head to the nearest downhill pool for a dip, although the best hiking is a stiff climb up the mountain to the upper pools through a vast bamboo forest and a fantastic world of waterfalls.

Getting to the lower pools is easy along a well-marked trail out of the parking area toward the flat, grassy peninsula. A series of pools lies off to the left and cool winds blowing off the sea make this a great spot for picnicking.

It is an amazing experience to lie in the lowest pool and look out to the waves crashing on the rocks only a few yards away. The best swimming down here can be found in the pools farther uphill, nearer the road, but you need to be careful. Fresh-water swimming can always be dangerous in Hawaii because of the sharp underwater rock formations.

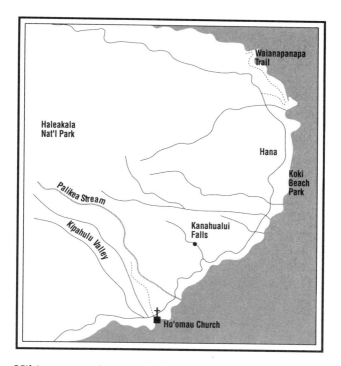

Hiking around even the lower pools involves some fairly difficult rock climbing. The most popular route is along the right side of the stream and the falls as the trail heads back toward the parking area.

You can climb to your heart's content amid some true wonders of nature. Once satisfied, head back to the road. The quickest way is along the left side of the embankment, leading over a bridge that offers the best view up and down this amazing valley.

The real treats, however, can be found by heading toward the higher elevations. The trail is named Waimoku Falls Trail after the most spectacular of the waterfalls. It can be reached by crossing the road at the parking lot and going through the gate into the nearby pasture. The two Waimoku Falls are about a half-mile up the back of the mighty volcano and are some two miles apart. Thankfully, the toughest part of the climb is at the beginning. The trail first heads to a fenced off scenic lookout with a clear view of the feathery Makahiku Falls. A few yards behind it, there is a well-worn, trench-like trail that leads to the edge of the falls and a truly gorgeous fresh-water pool. This is one place where you can swim safely to the very lip of the falls in the crystal clear fresh water.

That, however, is by no means the end of the trail. It continues through a lush grassy area that leads, incongruously, to a turnstile just before a wading pool and a path of hairpin turns up the other shore. You suddenly find yourself in a dense bamboo jungle and, when the wind is blowing, the vegetation whistles a sad and eerie song. The trail is well maintained as it winds its way through the green darkness. You emerge into a grove of mangoes and berries, and the trail again becomes well-marked. If you have come this far, it is worthwhile to follow the trail a ways further until at last it leads across a wooden walkway.

When you reach this point, you'll know what you have come for. The majesty of Waimoku Falls cascades over the mountains. It is so high that you have to strain your neck to see all the way to the top. There is a special spirit to this place and the waterfalls seem like a thread of silver stretching toward heaven. Surrounded by the sheer rock cliffs of a natural amphitheater, tiny rainbows appear and disappear as the sun dances like a leprechaun in the mist.

This part of the Haleakala National Park is free to campers with three-day permits, but close counts are not kept and a little stretching of the limit is seldom punished. The park rangers can point campers in the right direction to a large grassy area overlooking the Pacific and another view that few visitors who make it to this special and remote spot will ever forget.

The Seven Pools are remote, but they are not quite the end of the road. Route 31, the Hana Highway beyond Kipahulu, is truly rugged. It can be done in a rented car, though the car companies groan in dismay.

A mile and a half south of the pools is the Palupapa Hoomau Church, or St. Paul's, and the place where Charles Lindbergh is really buried. Pilgrims who remember the Lone Eagle's solo flight are drawn to the spot by the dreams of days gone by and the allure of a simpler time.

Hana itself is also worth walking around if you have the time. It is about as pretty a town as there is in Hawaii. For most visitors, it is only a stop on the way to the beach, but the more fortunate who stay or have no worries about time find more than enough to explore. The town is built on rolling hills that descend to the vast bay, with much of the surrounding land lush with pastures.

The true treasures of Hana are the beaches. Red Sand Beach, for example, is a fascinating and secluded place created by the eroded cinder lava of Haleakala and one of the best on the island for snorkeling.

Koki Beach Park is another mile out of town on the way to the Seven Pools. The riptides make swimming a bad idea, but it is ideally designed for beachcombing or as a one-night unofficial camping spot.

Between Koki and Hamoa are the remnants of an extensive Hawaiian fish pond, part of which survives from ancient times. The entire area is an eroding volcanic rim known as Kaiwi o Pele (bones of the volcano god).

It is clear that Hamoa Beach is nothing ordinary when you first spot it from the paved, torch-lined walkway. It is the semi-private beach attached to the Hotel Hana Maui, but it is open to the public because no beach can be closed in Hawaii.

Geographically, Hana and its surroundings are part of a lovely valley on the southeastern side of Maui. Historically, it was an ancient battleground in the wars of the Hawaiian chiefs. Physically isolated from the rest of Maui until the so-called highway was built in 1927, Hana is still largely untouched by the intrusions of the 20th century. The culture here remains basically Polynesian, which is part of its charm. The name refers to the spiritual force sought by the kings and queens of ancient Hawaii.

Old crafts are still a part of everyday life in Hana, and the local folk make beautiful flower leis, weave baskets and hats, husk coconuts, and pound poi using the original methods.

These are the simple attractions of Hana valley and its tiny port. It has drawn the rich and famous from all over the world and has a special charm for everyone who pays it a visit. Here they say "Ho'o kipa mai," which means come and be friendly. In Hana, it is an easy invitation to accept. The only thing to remember is that, if you are a visitor, you will want to spend more time than you had planned.

12

Kaanapali

Distance: 12 miles
Permit requirements: none
Rating: family

When visitors first see Kaanapali Beach, with its
beautiful views of the Pacific and the Neighbor Islands
of Molokai and Lanai, they understand why these
were dubbed the Islands of Paradise, and why the
name stuck for so long. The view makes the Pacific
seem more like a large lake than the largest body of
water in the world. The sunsets make wonderful
transitions from sun-filled days to fun-filled nights as
the sun sinks over the twinkling lights of Diamond
Head, urban Honolulu and the surrounding islands on
the horizon.

Most visitors to the Valley Isle make Kaanapali their
headquarters. Whether this is where you stay or not,
you should spend some time discovering its beauty
and exploring the better nearby hiking opportunities.

Nestled leeward of the 5,800-foot West Maui
Mountains, Kaanapali's broad beaches and cool lawns
were attracting visitors long before the first modern

hotel opened in 1963. Legend has it that royal families started visiting as early as 1100 AD.

The history of modern Kaanapali begins with the acquisition by Amfac Inc., one of Hawaii's largest companies, of Lahaina's Pioneer Mill and its lands by the beach. After decades as a loading site for sugar cane, the mill's board of directors authorized a study of land use in 1953. The result was one of the world's best known and most carefully planned resorts, begun in 1959. Today, 600 acres of Kaanapali Beach Resort's master-planned 1,200 acres have been developed as a tropical playground for visitors from all over the world.

But Kaanapali is only the beginning for exploring the Northwest Coast of Maui. Ten miles north is the Kapalua Resort, 750 of Maui's most beautifully carved acres at Fleming Beach, perhaps the only stretch of sand on the island giving Kaanapali any competition. Kapalua hosts two world-class hotels: Kapalua Bay Hotel & Villas and Ritz-Carlton Kapalua.

Before you head into the hills, the West Maui hiking you will probably enjoy most lies along the beaches. Kaanapali, also known as Hanakaoo, is the most famous and longest beach in the area. If you are not staying in one of the luxury beachfront hotels, it is easiest to park at Wahikuli State Park and walk along the beach to the Black Rock dividing the beach in two.

The entire area around the magnificent Black Rock is like an underwater marine park. The vast schools of reef fish, rays and turtles make it an extraordinary place for snorkeling.

If you want to avoid the price tag of Kaanapali, head for Honolowai and Kahana up the coast. They are both comfortable hikes from their glitzier neighbors to the south and north. Those in cars can take the Honoapiilani Highway, but hikers will want to walk along Lower Honoapiilani Highway through Honokowai and continue on to Yahana.

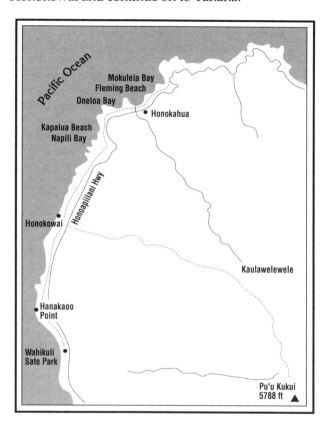

Honokawai Beach Park is right in Honokowai Town. It has a large lawn with palm trees and picnic tables, and a small beach with a tame surf for tots: Another safe one is Kahana. The splendid views of Molokai, Lanai and the South Coast of Oahu in the distance are outstanding.

At the northernmost end of the developed area, Kapalua sits like a crown atop Maui's crest. It beckons with some of the very best beaches on the Valley Isle. Hikers taking the Lower Honoapiilani sometimes think they are exploring the Greek Islands rather than the Polynesian Pacific. Two of the best beaches sit at the beginning of the route. Napili Bay is a perfect (but condo-lined) beach. There are lots of rights of way, though they are a little hard to find.

This is a great place for snorkeling and swimming, as well as for beginning surfers.

Kapalua Beach is another beautiful crescent beach that is seldom crowded. The public access is through a tunnel, and the well-formed reef hosts an extravagant fish life.

D. T. Fleming Beach is one of Maui's best; Oneloa Beach is small but offers great camping; Mokuleia hosts great body surfing; and Honolua Bay seems to be part of a beautiful world that time forgot. The beaches of Northwest Maui offer some great hiking opportunities if you are seeking the island's natural beauty, but the real hiking challenge lies in the hills.

Despite the wonder of Haleakala and the fame of the Iao Needle (thanks to Mark Twain), Puu Kukui is the most exhilarating and interesting trail on the island, and unquestionably the most difficult. It is only for brave souls who do not mind getting soaked to the skin and chilled to the bone by wind and rain – not exactly the Hawaii vacation experience most visitors have in mind.

Haelaau (meaning wild forest) House at the peak of Kaulalewelewe is the trailhead for the hike up Puu Kukui (candlenut hill). On a clear day, there are spectacular views of the west side of the island and of the offshore islands. The first few miles of the hike are through a thick forest with a wide variety of lush, green ferns. A few hundred feet farther on, there are three scenic lookouts near each other, with tremendous views of Honokahua Valley and its spectacular waterfall. From there to the summit, there is the most luxurient silversword growth in the Islands or in the world.

Some still insist that the only place in the world to discover silversword plants is on Haleakala, but they are found in these West Maui Mountains, and also on the slopes of Mauna Loa and Mauna Kea on the Big Island of Hawaii. In fact, there are three species, two of which are no longer endangered: the one in West Maui thrives on 200-300 inches of rain a year, and the other on Haleakala flourishes with only 16 to 50 inches on the barren slopes of Haleakala. The rarest of all is the greensword. It once flourished in the bog areas from 6,000 to 9,000 feet, but is rarely found now outside the mountains of West Maui. A few plants can also be found on the wet slopes of Haleakala, in the Kolau Gap and on the edge of the cliffs at Kaupo Gap. The main threat to the fragile species comes from feral goats and pigs wandering loose, especially on the slopes of Haleakala. The National Park Service deserves special credit for its tremendous efforts to save this endangered species.

Mark Twain and many other 19th-century visitors came up into these hills of West Maui. This was the route followed by the old horse trail, the only way in those days to travel from Kahului to Lahaina except by sea. But you can head even higher into the hills on the Puu Kukui Trail. On clear days, you will be rewarded with an overwhelming view of the Iao Valley, Central Maui, Haleakala, and the Big Island of Hawaii stretching up to and over the clouds on the horizon. The climb is worth the effort, though it can often be so damp that visibility is limited to four steps ahead.

The trip back will take less time because it is downhill. It is important to be cautious, however, because the hills can be wet and slippery and it is easy to lose your footing.

West Maui is the second most popular visitor destination in Hawaii today an,d for most, it is not hard to see why. Those seeking an escape from the 20th century, however, will be put off by all the hotel and condominium developments. But nature has left a mark on the area that the hand of man can't easily erase. For those in search of Hawaii the way nature meant it to be, West Maui still offers some of the richest rewards.

13

The Iao Valley State Park

Distance: 9 miles
Permit requirements: none
Rating: strenuous family

The Iao Valley has been a destination for pilgrims since ancient times, when it was one of the most sacred spots on Maui. Today, no visitor would dispute the fact that it is one of the most beautiful places to visit on the Valley Island.

The Iao Valley State Park is easy to reach on foot or by car and starts about three miles north of Wailuku. The county seat of Maui, Wailuku combines the old and new in ways that often leave visitors feeling they have discovered the incongruous reality of a tropical New England village.

The best way to explore the narrow, hilly streets of Wailuku is on foot. Many of the interesting old and new buildings are clustered in a compact area along High Street, between Main and Aupini Streets; even

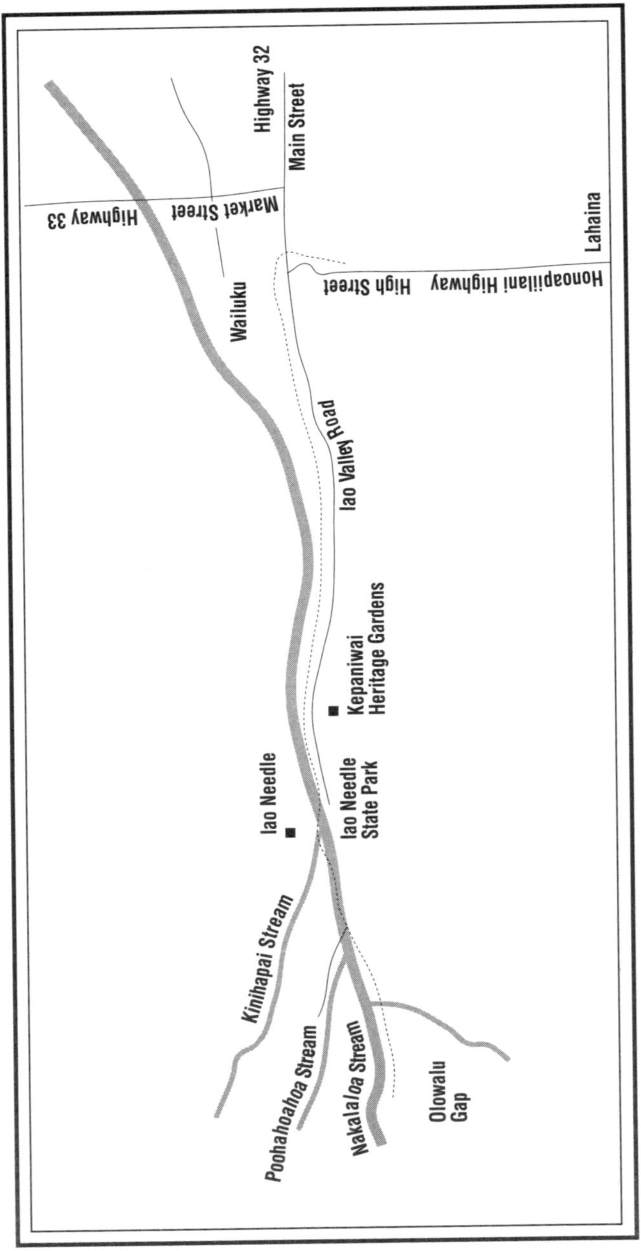
Highway 32
Main Street
Market Street
Highway 33
Lahaina
High Street
Honoapiilani Highway
Wailuku
Iao Valley Road
Kepaniwai
Heritage Gardens
Iao Needle
Iao Needle
State Park
Kinihapai Stream
Poohahoahoa Stream
Nakalaloa Stream
Olowalu
Gap

the names hint of Hawaii and New England together. The Wailuku Historic District is on the west side of High Street and it is easy to walk around the side streets to see older residential areas with small, tidy homes and colorful gardens reminiscent of Nantucket.

The hike to the State Park heads out of town along Wailuku's Main Street (Highway 32). Two miles out of town, it passes Kepaniwai Heritage Gardens, a Maui County Park with formal gardens and pavilions representing all of the cultures that have melted together to create the Hawaii of today. Richard C. Tong, a landscape architect, dreamed of and then created this park dedicated to all the people of Hawaii. It includes a thatch-roofed Hawaiian grass shack, a New England "salt box" home, a Japanese tea house with an authentic garden, a Chinese pagoda, and a Portuguese villa and garden with an outdoor oven.

The road ends in the Iao Valley State Park, dominated by the Iao Needle, a green-mantled remnant of an early eruption that rises sharply for 1,200 feet from the north valley floor. Mark Twain, with his usual understatement, called this spot the "Yosemite of the Pacific." The green carpet on the cliffs in the valley inspired Robert Louis Stevenson to coin a new word. He called it "viridescent" to describe the lush green vegetation seldom found outside Hawaii.

From the parking lot at the end of the road, it is easy to follow well-marked trails through an impressive collection of exotic trees and plants. You head down to the rushing stream, then up to a shelter for a panoramic view farther into the ravine, and finally to the top of the ridge for a commanding view of Kahului Bay, the valley floor, and the incredible Iao Needle.

The state park is an area for the whole family to enjoy, even though it is important to be careful when hiking off the trails because the mossy rocks of the West Maui Mountains can be treacherous. There are plenty of casual trails for the family, as well as more difficult hikes for the adventuresome.

A good trail for more ambitious hikers is the Tableland Trail, which starts out behind the Iao Needle lookout shelter. The first half-mile is steep and rises 500 feet above the shelter. Turning up a rough path to the left, the trail zig-zags along the ridge with a spectacular view of Iao Valley and Wailuku. The rest of the trail is a level walk through strawberry guavas, which are in season from August through October.

After returning to the parking lot, you can head down to the stream below for a swim to cool off. The chilly highland fresh water swimming is an experience few visitors to the islands expect.

There is another trail across the bridge at the parking lot which leads down the Iao Stream. This is a half-mile, well-marked trail along the stream, sometimes following the cliff above it until it ends abruptly at a large pool of fresh water. Hiking farther is difficult because there is no real trail but, for adventurous souls, it is possible to make your way down the stream bed.

About a mile below the parking lot, the stream divides. The relative seclusion and inviting pools have made this a favorite place for nude sunbathers and skinny dippers. To go even farther downhill following the Poohahoahoa Stream, will bring you to points so narrow in places that you have to swim or crawl over the rocks to proceed. This is a remote area where flash floods are not uncommon, so caution is advised and ropes are necessary. The trek through this beautiful natural area largely untouched by the hand of man is well worth the effort for those who are qualified and careful.

From the stream divide, Nakalaloa Stream is not as narrow or as dangerous as Poohahoahoa. There are a lot of large pools to swim in and a natural slide that drops into cool fresh water. Beyond that water slide, however, the terrain is rugged and the challenge should be taken only by the most seasoned hikers. For those who make the climb, it is necessary to traverse nearly vertical walls at some points, and it should not be tried alone or without rock climbing equipment.

With the right equipment it is possible to follow an old trail and pass through the mountains to Olowalu on their southwest side. This trail was used by ancient Hawaiians and offers a great chance to experience Hawaii the way nature intended it to be.

There is another brook, Kinihapai Stream, which flows on the west side of Iao Needle and under the bridge. Visitors are prohibited from hiking above the water intake, about a mile upstream. This is the water supply for Central Maui, and this is the most difficult stream to hike in the state park because of the slides that have come down the almost vertical walls. There is no trail, so the hike has to be made in the stream bed. Still the abundant wild fruits help make this another great walk.

Another hiking trail just outside Wailuku starts from Telephone No. 5. It is a vigorous hike for families, about an hour and a mile above the village. Permission must be obtained from the Wailuku Sugar Co. (tel. 244-7003).

In 1956, students from St. Anthony's High School in Wailuku erected a cross on a hill above the town. Today, there is an annual expedition to its successor for maintenance and repairs. The majority of the climb is straight uphill, but the breathtaking views of the Iao Valley make the hike well worthwhile. There are a lot of lookout spots along the way, giving you the chance to rest.

It is worth the added effort to climb up Kapilau Ridge for the dramatic views of the Iao Valley from above the cross. On a clear day, you can see the waterfalls and the mists they generate, as well as unobstructed panoramas of Central Maui and the southern stretch of the island beyond.

Kauai

14

Waimea Canyon

Kauai, the Garden Isle, is a lush emerald paradise in the middle of the Pacific. Many claim it is the most beautiful of all the Hawaiian Islands, but much of the island was devastated by Hurricane Iniki in September, 1992 and is still recovering.

Some of the most awesome spots look out on the Waimea Canyon, which Mark Twain, with his sense of modest description, called the "Grand Canyon of the Pacific." Part of Kokee State Park, it is a mile wide, over 10 miles long, and almost 4,000 feet deep. One of the popular pastimes at the lookouts is watching the shadows of clouds as they cross the chasm's walls. It is also one of the best places in Hawaii for hiking and offers more than 10 individual hiking trails.

Kokee State Park has 12 rustic cabins that are very popular with visitors and locals alike. Reservations are not required, but they are strongly recommended. Bring your own food, because the nearest store is in Kekaha, 20 miles away. There is also a privately-operated restaurant and bar a short walk from the cabins. Camp and trailer sites are available nearby on a picturesque shady field. Visits are limited to one week, but the facilities are free.

Hikes into Waimea Canyon or into the remote Alakai Swamp are full-day or overnight affairs, but there are a lot of relatively easy and short hikes available in the area of the park headquarters.

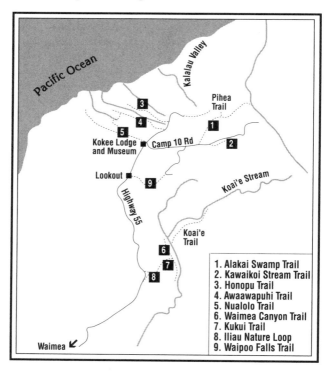

PIHEA TRAIL
Distance: 3½ miles

Permit requirements: none

Rating: strenuous

Pihea Trail is the newest in the Kokee area. It begins at the end of the highway, 3½ miles from the campground at Puu 0 Kila, overlooking Kalalau Valley. The first mile follows the remnants of a once-planned county roadway, abandoned in the face of loud opposition from environmentalists.

The views from the Kalalau Lookout give a breathtaking panorama of Hawaii untouched by man. It is usually also possible to see the white-tailed tropical birds soaring along the cliff walls through the valley. At an elevation of 4,000 feet, the impressive view from the lookout into the vast valley is a wonder to behold. Despite rumors you may hear, there is no trail down to the beach, and many hikers get into trouble thinking there is one.

The trail heads from the lookout over the rim of the valley to Pihea, the last lookout into Kalalau before entering the forbidding Alakai Swamp. The trail makes an abrupt turn as it goes into the swamp and then drops in and out of a number of valleys until it joins with the Alakai Swamp Trail.

From the juncture with the trail into the swamp, Pihea diverges again and meanders through native forests, crosses small streams, and winds through lush valleys until it reaches the north bank of Kawaikoi Stream. From there, it is an easy hike down the north side of the stream to Camp 10 Road.

ALAKAI SWAMP TRAIL
Distance: 3½ miles
Permit requirements: Division of Land and Forestry
Rating: strenuous

Hikers who make the trek agree that the Alakai Swamp is one of the most enchanting areas on the island. It is not for the fainthearted, however, and sturdy hiking boots are definitely in order.

The trailhead is at a marker on the Camp 10 Road, which can only be driven by four-wheel-drive vehicles and jeeps. It is well-maintained and the abandoned poles of an old military communications system mark the route.

After the first bog near the one-mile marker, the bogs start coming closer together and become deeper and wetter. The first two miles go up and down a number of fern-covered valleys, then the broad, flat expanse of the swamp spreads out before the trail where much of the vegetation has still not regrown following the devastation of Iniki.

At Kilohana Lookout there is a magnificent view into Wainha Valley – from the base of Mt. Waialeale to the sea beyond. Hanalei, the Bali Hai site in the movie *South Pacific*, lies beyond Wainiha and its wide deep bay is an enchanting place for resting up and picnicking.

AWAAWAPUHI TRAIL
Distance: 3½ miles
Permit requirements: Division of State Parks
Rating: strenuous

This is probably the best of the trails high into the mountains overlooking the astonishing Na Pali Cliffs. You should be in good physical condition before taking on this climb, and you should be prepared with a first aid kit, sturdy hiking boots, and fresh water.

The trailhead is at a telephone pole marked No. 14/2P/152 about half-way between Kokee Museum and the Kalalau Lookout. The trail descends into a humid forest, although it gets drier as it climbs the ridges above the valley. The only thing disturbing the hush of nature are the helicopters ferrying visitors who are unwilling to make the hike but still want to enjoy the breathtaking views. The trail is well maintained and there are numerous markers along the seven-mile loop, with an easy return along Nualolo Trail. The most sublime sight comes at a vertical perch high atop the Na Pali Cliffs. There may be no better spot on earth to enjoy a picnic and contemplate the wonder of what nature has created.

HONOPU TRAIL
Distance: 2½ miles
Permit requirements: Division of State Parks
Rating: strenuous

Like the Awaawapuhi Trail, Honopu takes hikers to tremendous lookouts for viewing the incomparable Na Pali Cliffs. It is not as well maintained, however, and slides along the cliff can make it dangerous in places.

It starts out a half-mile from the Awaawapuhi Trail north of Highway 55, weaves along a dry, forested area and then passes through scrub forests. There are a lot of lookout points for picnics and spectacular views into the Honopu Valley – Valley of the Lost Tribe of Hawaii. The remains of an ancient Polynesian village were found in this valley and have prompted much speculation about who the people were and what happened to them.

KAWAIKOI STREAM TRAIL
Distance: 2½ miles
Permit requirements: none
Rating: strenuous family

The trailhead is easy to find off the Camp 10 Road, but that is passable only by four-wheel-drive vehicles. It was created in 1975 when the Hawaii chapter of the Sierra Club and the Forest Service linked the Kawaikoi

Trail with the Pihea Trail. The path follows the south side of the stream along an easy and well-marked trail through lush vegetation. There are several swimming holes along the way, and many feel this is the most beautiful area of Kauai.

NUALOLO TRAIL
Distance: 3½ miles
Permit requirements: none
Rating: strenuous

This is the easiest of the three trails to the Na Pali Cliffs. It sets out between the ranger station and the cabins in Kokee and makes a seven-mile loop, with some of the most awe-inspiring panoramas in the Hawaiian Islands.

After passing through a lush, cool forest, the trail descends 1,500 feet to spectacular lookouts over Nualolo Valley. Food and water need to be carried because neither is available in this backwater of nature.

KOAIE CANYON TRAIL
Distance: 3 miles
Permit requirements: none
Rating: difficult

This is a favorite with most backpackers and hikers, leading to a secluded wilderness shelter. The trailhead is easy to find if you hike north along the Waimea River. It goes on to follow the south side of Koaie Stream into the canyon.

The fertile valley was once intensely farmed and it is still easy to see the abundant terraces and former house sites. There is an open shelter, Lonomea Camp, at the end of the trail where the Lonomea tree – it grows only on Kauai and Oahu – reaches heights up to 30 feet.

WAIMEA CANYON TRAIL
Distance: 1½ miles
Permit requirements: none
Rating: strenuous

This is another popular trail, but is more difficult than the Koaie Canyon Trail. It heads north through the heart of the canyon to the junction of Koaie Stream and the Waimea River.

The trail is well maintained and leads up the valley on the west side of the river to a maintenance man's house. It can be reached by hiking up seven miles from Waimea, or by hiking down the Kukui Trail, though the latter is exhausting and requires permission.

KUKUI TRAIL
Distance: 2½ miles
Permit requirements: none
Rating: strenuous

This is a short trail into the beautiful Waimea Canyon. A Forestry Division sign marks the trailhead just off the Iliau Trail. Visitors are allowed to spend up to three nights here.

The first part of this well-maintained trail drops sharply down 2,000 feet into the canyon. It includes some spectacular views of Waialae Falls across the gorge to the east and of Waimea Canyon.

The second portion passes through heavy undergrowth and emerges at Wiliwili Camp. It is a delightful place to camp in the cool shade, with plenty of fresh water from the stream. Many visitors make this their base camp and then explore the spur route throughout the canyon. Nevertheless, it is possible to hike in and out in a single day if you are in good physical condition.

ILIAU NATURE LOOP
Distance: ¼ mile
Permit requirements: none
Rating: family

This hike through nature is a great way to see some 20 native species of plants, most of which are marked with identifying plates. The main attraction, however, is the unique and rare Iliau plant. The trail offers a number of spectacular views of the Waialae Falls on the opposite side of the canyon.

WAIALAE CANYON TRAIL
Distance: 1½ miles
Permit requirements: none
Rating: strenuous

Although this trail is steep, it offers some of the finest views of the Waimea Canyon. It begins off the Kukui Trail, involving a short hike, and first emerges a quarter-mile out on the east rim of Waimea Canyon. It snakes along the sheer cliff and then heads into a gulch, following the cliffs to Waipoo Falls, a great place for a picnic or a cool swim. From the falls, there is a steep climb up the mountains with many lookouts into the canyon.

Whichever trails you pick, there is an awesome beauty to the Waimea Canyon you will never forget. You can spend as much time as you want exploring here but the Na Pali Cliffs still beckon – and they offer an even more incredible series of sights, perhaps the most spectacular Hawaii has to offer.

15

Kalalau Valley & The Na Pali Cliffs

THE KALALAU TRAIL
Distance: 22 miles (round trip)
Permits: required for the Hanakapiai, Hanakoa and
Kalalau Valleys from the Division of State Parks
Rating: difficult

The Kalalau Trail is very different from its Waimea Valley cousin, yet it still hosts some of the most spectacular views in the Hawaiian Islands. The Kalalau Valley stretches more than 4,000 feet up from the Pacific Ocean.

Once they have seen the Kalalau Valley, visitors have no questions about why Kauai was nicknamed the Garden Isle. On the sides of this spectacular stretch of green the etched mountains rise out of the sea, with waterfalls cascading into the valley floor. The lookout peers down the Kalalau Valley to the sea and, dividing the valley from the mighty blue Pacific beyond, you can see a tiny ribbon of sand. The Kalalau Trail traces this sandy stretch over 10 miles back and forth through one of the most incredible areas of beauty nature ever created. It can be reached by following Route 56 to the end of the road, 38 miles out of Lihue.

When hikers talk about exploring Kauai, they are usually talking about seeing the uninhabited valleys of this Na Pali Coast. The Kalalau Trail to the beach at the end of the cliffs is the most exhilarating walk on the island.

Until a few years ago, the Kalalau Valley was privately owned by the Robinson family, who have controlled much of Kauai and the nearby but forbidden island of Niihau for generations. The valley, beach, and Na Pali coastal lands, however, are now under the control and management of the Division of State Parks.

No one who has ever hiked the Kalalau Trail would deny its incredible grandeur. The cliffs rise sharply out of the emerald blue ocean from the beautiful secluded beaches. The valleys of the Na Pali Coast are accessible only by foot or boat, although it is possible to take an airborne look by helicopter. The trail is well maintained, but the frequent slides and fallen trees can make it hazardous in places and caution is advised.

Hiking the entire length of the trail requires backpacking equipment. It is also possible for the less adventuresome to explore only the first mile to get an idea of what they are missing – and why they should come back at least once more for another look.

Sturdy hiking boots are essential to deal with the soft volcanic cinders on the coast and the rocky trails up into the valleys. Another necessity is a sturdy, water-proof tent to deal with the rain in Hanakoa and the winds at Kalalau.

The bay at Waikoko on the eastern end of the Lumahai shore is one of the most photographed sights in the

Islands. A trail descends the cliffs from the scenic lookout on the highway to a small cove which is ideal for picnicking and windsurfing. The Haena region was once densely settled, but today it is filled with vacation cottages. Kee Beach, the location for filming the TV drama *The Thornbirds,* is quiet and peaceful, but is not usually safe for swimming.

Hikers get their first glimpse of the sublime Na Pali Cliffs from the northern end of Kee Beach. The lush cliffs rise 3,000 feet straight out of the sea over a series of deep, jungled valleys stretching all the way to Mana.

The hike to Hanakapiai Beach is about a mile straight up and another down from Kee Beach. This is the most popular part of the trail because tourist publications promise a lush valley with plenty of native plant life. Fear not! No one is ever disappointed. The first half-mile of the climb offers some spectacular views back to Kee Beach and Haena. The trail is cool and shady here because of the large trees and tradewinds. The up-and-down trail from the half-mile marker to the quarter-mile marker is well maintained and easy to hike. Near the one-mile marker, there is a rare spring that beckons with thirst-quenching water.

The thrills really begin at the half-mile marker and the first view of Hanakapiai Beach below, with its broad sands and thundering surf. The Hanakapiai Loop Trail branches off about half-way down to the beach. It is a two-mile hike to the base of Hanakapiai Falls. The hike to the falls and a swim in the Hanakapiai Stream is usually warm and sunny in the afternoons, when it seldom rains.

Hanakapiai Beach is the only place in the area with campsites and is good for overnighting. There is a camping area on the beach (besidef the stream) and two Division of Forestry shelters about a half-mile from the beach.

Out of Hanakapiai, the trail climbs sharply and does not drop to the sea again until it reaches Kalalau Beach. The footing is sure, but it is all up and down and the weather is usually hot.

Hanakoa, about six miles from Hanakapiai, is a good place to stop for a rest. There is a path leading from a rustic cabin to a wonderful waterfall with its own swimming pool in the Hanakoa Stream. Along the hike from Hanakapiai to Kalalau, there is a good deal of nudity. The Eden-like setting and splendid climate seem to make inhibitions disappear and you will discover there are a lot of people in good shape on Kauai.

The Hanakapiai Loop is an easy climb along the stream and through a rainforest filled with abundant vegetation. "Okolehau" is a Division of Forestry trail-crew shelter near the abandoned coffee mill, but visitors can use it when it is not occupied by a trail crew.

The hike up Hanakapiai Falls from the valley should not be missed because the falls are spectacular and the valley is serene and enchanting. Don't try it, however, if the water in the stream is too deep for crossing at any point. The trail is easy to follow as it cuts through the cliffs of the very narrow canyon. At the end of the climb, the Hanakapiai Falls cascade 300 feet over the cliffs into a dark but inviting natural pool.

Really serious hiking begins at Kalalau as it climbs out of the Hanakapiai Valley over a series of switchbacks. Morning hiking is best with the sun ever at your back and constant, cool tradewinds.

The first valley is Hoolulu, a crack in the mountain thick with vegetation. Because the trail narrows where the cliffs are steepest and there are sometimes rock slides, caution is warranted.

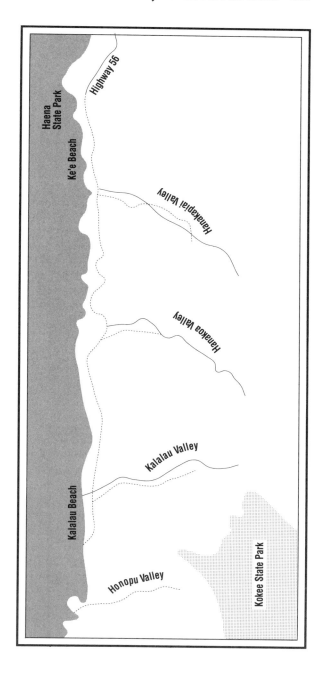

Four more miles out along the coast is the Waiahuakua Valley. It is broader than Hoolulu and, in summer, is alive with delicious mountain apple trees. The first view of Waiahuakua Valley unfolds at the 4¼-mile marker. It too is broad, and it is terraced, having once been farmed by Hawaiians. The terraces and trail-crew shelters offer good places for camping. Although the afternoons can be sunny, it rains a lot here and one shower is almost immediately followed by the next.

The stretch of the trail from Hanakoa to Kalalau is the severest test for the skill and conditioning of hikers. Caution is important because of the switchbacks, which alternately climb and descend the steep cliffs. There are often slides along the way. But it is well worth the effort because there are few sights in all the world to compare with what you will see from this trail. The views of the northwest coastline are staggering, especially against a setting sun.

Near the six-mile marker the trail enters land that was part of the Makaweli cattle ranch until 1975. There are not as many markers in this area, but it is impossible to get lost because the trail is so visible over the open land.

The last small valley before Kalalau is called Pohakuao. This is where hikers get their first clear view of the sublime Kalalau Valley. This is a unique site. The broad valley is three miles long and two miles across. From the ridge, there is a precipitous trail dropping to the Kalalau Stream, where the rushing creek and its pools make the setting cool and serene.

Camping is only permitted on the beach, among the trees along the beach, and in the caves at its far end. It is best to find a spot offering shelter from the strong winds and hot daytime sun. Guava are plentiful and make rich additions to picnics in season. The waterfalls by the caves at the end of the beach are a terrific place for a natural shower.

The best trail in the spectacular valley sets out on the west side of the Kalalau Stream at a well-marked trailhead. The remains of an ancient temple are clearly visible near the starting point, but remember that such sites are revered by many native Hawaiians.

Smoke Rock, at the one-mile point, is a great place to stop and take in the panoramic view of the entire valley. The rest of the hike to Big Pool is shaded and cool, and the smooth slide connecting the two room-sized pools here will give you a wonderful ride.

A group of enterprising scouts cut a trail from Kalalau Stream to Davis Falls in 1984. The falls are the best place on the coast to swim and to enjoy the sights and aromas of Kalalau-Kauai's most precious jewel.

Some visitors use the dry caves on the beach for camping, but everyone wades and splashes in the wet caves. In the summer, a few half-wade and half-swim to neighboring Honopu, the legendary "Valley of the Lost Tribe." The remains of an ancient native Hawaiian settlement from which inhabitants inexplicably disappeared have been unearthed. Extreme caution is encouraged because picking your way around the point on foot can be treacherous.

Beyond Kalalau Valley, the sheer cliffs of the Na Pali Coast are inaccessible by land. Visitors generally have to content themselves with the stunning views from Kee Beach, or else hire one of the popular helicopter tours flying visitors along the indescribable coast.

16

Hanalei Bay

Distance: 15 miles
Permit requirements: none
Rating: family

There is an overwhelming feeling to the peaceful
beauty of Hanalei Bay. The bay itself is a long crescent
of sandy beach etched into the half-moon base of
intricately carved mountains. It stretches from
Kolokolo Point and its Lumahai Beach, where Mitzi
Gaynor vowed to "Wash That Man Right Out of My
Hair" to Puu Poa Point, where Rossano Brazzi sang
"Some Enchanted Evening." Most visitors recognize it
as the setting for the movie *South Pacific*. Despite
having none of the cliffs of the Waimea Canyon or the
Na Pali Coast, the vast valley offers great
opportunities for hiking and camping in one of
Hawaii's most beautiful spots.

Many hikers start out in Princeville because that is
where they are staying. This was the site of a
19th-century coffee plantation started in 1853 and
converted to a resort in 1969. Ultimately, it will be the
largest resort on Kauai, with 11,000 acres. Sitting atop
Kauapea Beach (also called Secret Beach for visiting

mainlanders), it offers a breathtaking panorama of the vast expanse of Hanalei Bay.

Kauapea Beach is a special place that feels forgotten by time. Hikers' footsteps are likely to be the only ones along this little-visited strand.

Getting here is half the fun, and the trailhead is easy to find by a small, weathered sign marked "Beach Trail." The hike is steep, but there are plenty of natural handholds and once you reach the sea there is great beach walking.

The Hanalei National Wildlife Refuge is on the other side of the resort. Visitors are not allowed out of their cars except at the Haraguchi Rice Mill Museum and on the trail at the end of the road just beyond the refuge.

The narrow little bridges in and out of Hanalei and the village of Waioli have set them apart, undisturbed by most of the 20th century. This remote outpost was settled by missionaries in the 19th century, but today residents are primarily wealthy escapists and members of the counterculture left over from the '70s.

The area north of the Wildlife Refuge on the way to the Na Pali Cliffs is free of tour buses, thanks to those little bridges which must be crossed to reach it. The spectacular bay itself is world famous and the fitting end of several Trans-Pacific Cup races from California. In summer months when the water is smooth, the bay is home to a flotilla of yachts and brightly painted boats around the single pier under the cliffs of Princeville. A park near the marina and another half-way around the bay have small parking lots as well as picnic areas and bathrooms. Every street leads to the bay, and the weather-beaten buildings and quaint churches make it an ideal place to explore on foot. The most interesting sight in the village is the Waioli Mission House, a prefab shipped from New England and built in 1836 by the Wilcox family. It has been restored, refurnished to the period, and hosts the most extensive quilt collection in Hawaii. Quilts in the tropics may sound strange, but the north shore of Kauai can be as chilly as New England.

The nearby Waioli Mission Hall, with its unrestored bell tower, was built in 1841. The church originally had a thatched roof and a pebble floor.

There are some shops in Waioli, a small modern shopping center for picking up supplies, and the last gas station in this part of the island. The century-old Ching Young Store Kauaiians talk about, however, is now the Native Trading and Cultural Center and it is primarily a museum.

Because of the absence of tour vehicles, the "highway" is ideal for hiking as well as driving. The north bend out of town is heavily planted in pines, and the brisk tradewinds make it feel more like northern California than the tropics, even in the dog days of August.

The first beach that hikers reach after Makahoa Point is Hahalahala Beach. This stretches from the point to a spit of black rocks. The beach is famous as the "Nurse's Beach" in *South Pacific.* Just beyond the rocks is Lumahai Beach, one of the most beautiful beaches on Kauai, and the setting for "Bali Hai" in the same movie.

There is a steep trail down through the thick pandanus trees to the beach itself. Swimming here should only be attempted in summer when the water is calm; even then, the undertow and tricky currents can make it dangerous.

There is a stream at the western end of Lumahai Beach where the cold fresh water from the mountains crashes into the ocean, sending beautiful sprays into the air. It is also a beautiful beach for walking and the coarse sand makes a great workout for the legs.

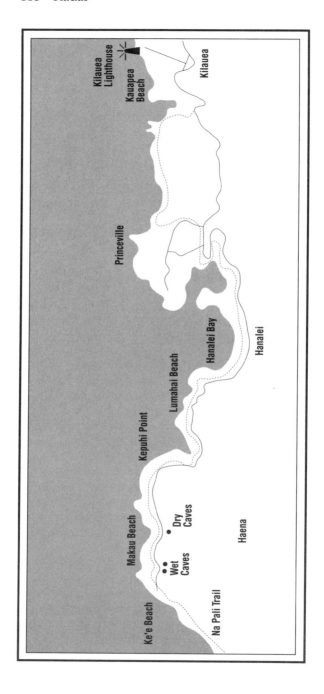

Another cold, fresh-water stream winds across Haena Beach Park's golden sand with its dazzling blue water. An offshore reef makes this a good place for snorkeling and rafting in summer.

The Haena area was once heavily settled, but today it is sprinkled thinly with vacationers' cottages and oldtimers' homes. The Wainiha General Store offers limited supplies and the Hanalei Colony Resort hosts a restaurant (Charo's), bar, and art gallery. Just past the store are two narrow bridges in an idyllic setting. The "temporary" structures here were built in 1957 when a tsunami (or typhoon) wiped out their predecessors. Just beyond lies Powerhouse Road. The road meanders two miles inland through a lush valley, past waterfalls, heiaus (ancient temples), perfectly preserved taro terraces, and ancient homesites. It dead-ends at a powerhouse and the trailhead for Powerhouse Trail – a good climb into the hills.

Another trail leads to the west at the base of the Wainiha Valley and links up with the Alakai Swamp Trail after 2½ miles (see Chapter 14).

Hiking or driving farther out the main road to Kepuhi, you will find a dramatic view – including a powerful blowhole. All of the beautiful beaches in the area, however, are dangerous and not for swimming.

Beyond that is Makua Beach, called "Tunnels" by the surfers because of the wave formations caused by the large break between the two reefs. Snorkeling inside the reef is good most of the time, but it is *breathtaking* on calm summer days, when it is even possible to venture safely outside the reef. This is another place where you can bring a supply of frozen peas or some bread crumbs to attract the extravagant schools of tropical fish. Snorkeling in the coral formations is exciting: thousands of fish in the brightest colors of the rainbow will swim up to eat from your hands.

There is a cluster of homes on the mountain side of the road just past Makua Beach. The descendants of the last native Hawaiians to live in Kalalau Valley live there today.

From here, Haena Beach extends from the point until it disappears west of Haena Beach Park with its three sets of caves. The first is Maniniholo Dry Cave, the end of an old lava tube running several hundred yards under the cliffs; it was about twice as large until 1957, when the tsunami half-filled it with sand. Another mile out the road are the Waikipalae and Waikanaloa Wet Caves. Legend has it that Pele, the volcano goddess, dug but abandoned them when she found not fire but water.

Even if you choose not to hike the Na Pali Cliffs, you should drive to the end of the road, where the trail starts out. The beach and the nearby views of the cliffs are hard to absorb when you see them for the first time.

As with most beaches on the North Shore, the conditions at Kee Beach vary with the time of year. Winter swells can easily reach 20 feet, with the giant rollers crashing into the shore. In summer, snorkeling can be spectacular near the reef, although it will feel ice cold along the surface from the rainwater. Even in the shallows where you can stand up in the sun-warmed waters, it will be colder than you expect. In summer it can be perfectly still and so clear that bubbles on the surface cast long shadows on the sandy bottom.

This spot was the backdrop for some of the scenes in the TV drama *The Thornbirds,* which starred Richard Chamberlain. "It's so simple in Hawaii," he says. "Watching the sunset is the big event of the day."

If you are still at Kee by the end of the day, or if you are spending the night, make the short trek back to Kee Lagoon. The view of the sun slowing settingwill be spectacular, perhaps equalled only by the setting sun on Kauai's southern shores at Poipu.

17

Poipu

Distance: 10 miles
Permit requirements: none
Rating: family

The ancient monarchs knew how to pick resort locations. They lived in Waikiki when it was still in its pristine splendor, they lived in Lahaina before the first whalers arrived, and then they settled at Poipu on the shimmering South Shore of Kauai.

Visitors are now following in their footsteps to Poipu Beach, one of Hawaii's most popular resorts. It is built along two miles of crescent-shaped beaches, with sparkling white sand and a calm turquoise sea. The sun almost always shines, but the northerly tropical breezes keep it cool and dry.

To reach this shore, head out of Lihue, with its airport and megamodern resorts, on Route 50. Turn south on Route 52, which branches off toward Old Koloa Town and the area surrounding Poipu Beach. It is possible to hike it, but the roads are long, dry and uninteresting.

Life here today centers around the sun, but it has not always been that way. In earlier days, the area played host to King Sugar, and some picturesque old plantation towns and mills still stand among the cane fields, mostly fast-disappearing relics of history.

Hawaii's sugar industry began in Koloa, with the establishment of the first commercial plantation in 1835. Koloa Landing was once the third port of the Hawaiian Islands, after Honolulu and Lahaina, Maui. This is the spot where Captain James Cook discovered the Sandwich Islands in 1778. The first Roman Catholic mission in Hawaii was established in Koloa in 1841, and it built St. Raphael's stone church in 1856. The White Church was built by an early Protestant missionary in 1837 and remodeled in 1929, when it opened to visitors.

Koloa lies beneath spreading banyans, with a stream running through it. A gas station, a general store, and many other buildings have been standing there longer than anyone can remember and they have all been faithfully and lovingly restored.

Leading out of Koloa, Route 53 takes visitors into the hills to The Pacific Tropical Botanical Garden, the only one of its kind chartered by Act of Congress as a research station to save endangered native plants. Hikers can admire rare and beautiful plants on its lush 186 acres. The much smaller Olu Pua Garden nearby is also worth visiting. It is a former plantation manager's estate now open as a botanical garden. All these sights on the South Shore are within easy hiking distance for intrepid enthusiasts.

Also in the hills above Koloa is the Waita Reservoir, the largest in Hawaii. At 425 acres, the lake is also the largest in the Hawaiian Islands. It was considered a modern engineering miracle when completed in 1906. Today, it is a good place for fishing and digging for clams.

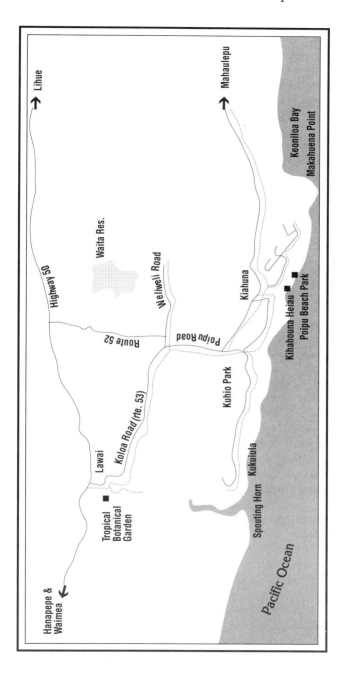

When Hector and Alexandra Moir lived in Poipu in the 1930s, they started an unusual garden of cacti and succulents on their six-acre estate. Today, it is the first thing visitors see after entering Poipu and, since they opened a restaurant in 1968, it has been a popular place for dining.

Getting to the area on foot or by car can be confusing, but it is not hard to find. To reach the Poipu beaches, follow Poipu Road. It passes Poipu Beach Park and ends at Makahuena Point.

There is plenty to do at Poipu. Water sports abound and, when visitors tire of them, there is golf, tennis, bike riding, whale-watching (November to May), and gallery snooping.

After a stroll through the Moir Gardens, it is an easy walk down past the Sheraton Kauai and the Kiahuna complex. Crescent-shaped Kiahuna Beach is open to the public and absolutely spectacular with its white sand, clear skies, and cool tradewinds. Swimming and snorkeling are always safe because of the offshore reef, and some of the best board-surfing sites on the island are found here.

The Kihouna Heiau (ancient temple) has been restored in front of the Waiohai Resort. It can be disappointing today, but when Captain Cook found the place, he described its walls as four to six feet tall in a rectangle measuring 130 by 100 feet.

Heading east along never-crowded Poipu Road and turning makai (toward the sea) on Hoowili Road takes hikers to Poipu Beach Park, a pleasant four-acre spot with restrooms, showers, and covered picnic areas. The beach is always safe and is one of only two on Kauai with full-time lifeguards. This is one of a series of great beaches, each with its own specialty. The next one (heading east) is Brennecke's Beach, the home of Dr. Marvin Brennecke until the state expropriated it for public use in 1976. It was the best in Hawaii for body surfing until Hurricane Iwa struck in 1982, and it is still the best on Kauai for board surfing. But the loss of sand in the hurricane and the presence of large rocks makes it rough for body surfing.

It is an easy hike out a cane road east to Keoniloa Bay, the site of a luxury 506-room Hyatt Regency resort opened in 1991. The beach is open to the public. Shipwreck Beach here was never much to talk about before Iwa hit, but the hurricane blasted the South Shore and created a new shoreline. The old narrow sliver of sand is now an enormous golden strand divided by lava rocks. To the left of the rocks, the wide, gleaming sand stretches all the way to the base of the South Shore's low cliffs and some beautiful sand dunes. To the right, waves roll across a long, shallow reef helping to protect the shore.

Although Shipwreck Beach is not safe for swimming, it is wonderful for walking, running, or exercising – especially near the waterline. You can also climb the cliffs to explore their eerie caves and rock formations.

The lucky few who continue along the cane road two more miles, where it dead-ends on a second east-west road, have the chance to explore another spectacular beach, Mahaulepu. This beach, however, is on land owned by the McBryde Sugar Company so their permission is required.

To explore the rest of Poipu, head east on Lawai Road. Actually, the coast has traditionally been called Kukuiula, but it is coming to be seen as part of the wonderful area known as Poipu.

Kuhio Park guards the shallow and completely protected Hoona Beach, probably the best beach on Kauai for children. Farther down the road is Keiki (child) Beach, beckoning with a totally protected pond, where toddlers cannot wander away because of its surrounding walls.

Farther along Lawai Road is Kukuiula Harbor and Kukuiula Beach, always clean and safe except during severe Kona storms. This was the site of an old Hawaiian fishing pond but the last remnant was wiped out by Hurricane Iwa, along with all the homes then in the area.

Finally, at the end of the well-paved portion of the road is Spouting Horn Park. The high waves force air and water out of the opening of an ancient lava tube, producing a moaning sound and a jet spray.

No visit to the South Shore of Kauai is complete without a hike to or around Hanapepe, "The Biggest Little Town on Kauai." This was where the in-town scenes of Australia were shot for the TV program, *The Thornbirds.* The road through town, following the winding Hanapepe River, is reminiscent of the Old West in America as well. Intriguing wooden buildings hanging out over the river bank, a narrow old bridge crossing the stream, and the farms on the old road give visitors a good idea of what it was like here in early rural Hawaii.

In and around the village of Waimea, the former Polynesian capital of the island and the commercial center of Southwest Hawaii today (with a population of 1,500), there is not a lot to see except for the remains of an old Russian Fort built in 1817 by a crazy German doctor. Also a former Moscow policeman, he was named Georg Anton Scheffer. Scheffer built a Russian fort in Honolulu, where the Aloha Tower now stands, and two more on Kauai's North Shore in the vain hope of enticing a Russian invasion of the Islands.

This shore is just about the only place in Hawaii for catching a glimpse of Niihau, the Forbidden Isle, 17 miles across the sea. It has been privately owned by the Robinson family since 1864 and visitors are not welcome. But the family has recently made it possible to fly over for a glimpse by helicopter tour.

The area is also the starting point for any excursion into the incredible Waimea Canyon. Compared with other parts of Hawaii, it remains fairly remote and little visited.

Molokai

18

Kalaupapa

Distance: 4 miles
Permit requirements: none to hike, but it is necessary
to arrange to be met by an authorized tour operator at
the base of the trail
Rating: strenuous

Kalaupapa is unique. For years it has been used as a
leper colony, which explains why Molokai used to be
called "The Lonely Island." In the old days, this was a
cursed place, a kind of living death. Starting in the
1860s, sufferers from Hansen's Disease were pushed
off boats at a point called Makanalua, "the given
grave," to live in neglect and isolation at Kalawao on
the eastern side of the Kalaupapa peninsula. Thanks
to medical science, leprosy has been controlled and
visitors can travel to this bittersweet spot without
danger to their health.

"They were strangers to each other," wrote Robert
Louis Stevenson, "collected by common calamity,
disfigured, mortally sick, banished without sin from
home and friends.... In the chronicle of man, there is
perhaps no more melancholy landing than this."

Father Damien de Veuster, a young Belgian priest, came to this place of great natural beauty to minister to the lepers' spiritual and physical needs in 1873. Damien was an outstanding carpenter and he built several churches, the last of which was St. Philomena in Kalawao, completed shortly before he too succumbed to the disease a century ago.

Richard Marks, the local sheriff who was originally taken there 30 years ago as a "patient," and the U. S. Government are creating the newest National Historic Park here. Marks and his wife Sara, also a victim, still live there today, along with about 80 other survivors.

The Kalaupapa National Historical Park was formally established in 1980, but it is still in its formative stages today. It is dedicated to preserving the memories of the past, providing a well-maintained community for the present residents, and educating present and future generations around the world about a disease that has been shrouded in ignorance and fear for centuries.

The project includes restoration of the little St. Philomena Church. Its simple but elegant lines gave the community a focus and an ideal for a new way of living. It is used infrequently now, but is considered the most significant building on the peninsula by the National Park Service and the Catholic Diocese of Honolulu.

Sister Richard Marie, a nurse at Kalaupapa since 1960, may have described it best. "The people here seem to appreciate what we do for them more than anywhere else.... Really, I feel privileged that I have been here these years. I don't know how to explain it, but I am not worried about outside things. I think this is a little bit of heaven."

Today, Kalaupapa is a peaceful, New England-like village with the sleepy streets of a happy hamlet, but it is one of the few settlements on earth which cannot be reached by automobile. This sleepy backwater where people seldom hurry beckons with the most spectacular seaside cliffs in Hawaii. Still, outsiders are only allowed if accompanied by Mr. Marks or the one other authorized guide. Kalaupapa unveils the Hawaii of a century ago and what life was like in quieter times, earning for itself the nickname of the Friendly Island.

High on a windy ridge in Palaau, overlooking the peninsula, is the Kalaupapa Lookout. The sheer cliff formed a geological barrier that isolated the peninsula from the rest of Molokai. In 1886, Manuel Joao Garinha, an immigrant from Madeira, carved a narrow three-mile trail into the cliff for mules to transport supplies and cattle to the settlement below. Today, visitors can travel down the 1,600-foot precipice to visit the peninsula itself.

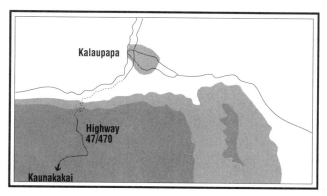

It is an easy drive from the airport to the entrance of Palaau State Park and the trailhead. The park includes a fine camping area for hikers spending the night.

Before the descent, walk over to the Kalaupapa Lookout. It offers a beautiful panorama of one of the most spectacular seaside sights on earth. The view takes in the 3,000-foot cliffs of the inaccessible North Shore. The *Guinness Book of World Records* calls them the highest sea cliffs in the world, and the view is one of the most dramatic in Hawaii.

A shorter trail of 150 yards traverses a dense, evergreen forest. A 10-minute hike takes you through the eucalyptus trees to a famous natural stone formation called the Phallic Rock. In ancient times, barren women are said the have made pilgrimages to this sacred rock to pray for conception.

At the sign by the entrance to the park is another trail to the original Kalaupapa Overlook. The road can be muddy, especially during the rainy season, but the different angle offers a more dramatic view than the one from the newer scenic lookout. The North Shore cliffs cannot be seen from here, but the trailhead of the century-old Kalaupapa is obvious.

In earlier days this was also known as the Jack London Trail, named after the famous author who wrote about it in one of his short stories. The trail itself is wide and safe despite the abrupt descent and 25 hairpin turns, although it is easy to twist an ankle in a hole left by the mules. They start making the hike every morning at 8:30. It is coolest in the early morning, but the shade and tradewinds keep it comfortable all year round. Along the way, there are a host of wonderful views of the remote little peninsula, which was formed by the eruption of a "shield volcano" long after the rest of the island had been formed. There is a mule corral at its base, and you are allowed to proceed no further until you have been met by your guide, although it is possible to simply return "topside." To do so, however, would be to miss an experience many find one of the most emotional in all of Hawaii.

The tour includes a hike or bus ride reminiscent of *Night of the Iguana* to the eastern end of the peninsula. This was where the first lepers were sent and was the home of the colony for Father Damien and the other victims long after his death.

The sharp cliffs plunging into the sea and the stark offshore islands make this a place of overwhelming natural beauty very few people ever see. When a water pipeline made it possible, the population shifted to what is today the town of Kalaupapa on the drier leeward side of the peninsula.

"When we first came here, we looked at the mountains and saw a prison," according to Paul, a long-time resident. Approximately 100 "patients" still live here, but largely out of sentimental attachment to the place, since there is no longer a valid medical reason to keep the victims of the disease isolated from the rest of the world.

There is not much to see in the town of Kalaupapa other than the settlement, the wharf where barges land twice a year, the air station servicing the Piper Cubs that bring in visitors, and the fine beaches with their rough surf. A visit to the peninsula and the little town it hosts, however, will never be forgotten.

19

Halawa

Distance: 5 miles
Permit requirements: none
Rating: family

There is another tremendous hike through an even more remote site on Molokai and that is to the waterfalls high in the Halawa Valley at the easternmost end of the Friendly Isle. No one lives here today, and the road in is long, steep and difficult. But it is an experience vnot to be missed.

It is also possible to hike out the road from Kaunakakai to the far end of the island. It is a long walk, but there is a lot to see and do along the way. You might want to take it in segments, since the whole trek is too much for a single visit. The complete absence of traffic makes it unlike any roadside walk you will ever take on the Mainland. The first sight out of the town is the Kalokoeli Fishpond, the first remnant of a complex system of aquaculture ponds that extends most of the way along the Southern Coast. In ancient times, there were at least 62 individual ponds. Many were built in the 13th century and they were under the command of the Hawaiian chiefs for their own use. The fish ponds were built in the sea using curved walls of stone or by building a single straight connecting wall between two points of land. Openings with grilled gates were constructed at certain points so as to assure the best circulation of sea water. These ponds were stocked with fish, which were harvested with nets when needed.

Kawela is another two miles out the road. It covers a large area rich in history, including the remains of chiefs' residences, other house ruins, petroglyphs, burial sites, and caves.

A fortress was built high on a steep, inaccessible ridge in the middle of the gulch. King Kamehameha I fought a battle here for control of the island in the late 18th century, and oral tradition contends that the fortification was also used as a place of refuge or sanctuary for those who were about to be used for human sacrifice.

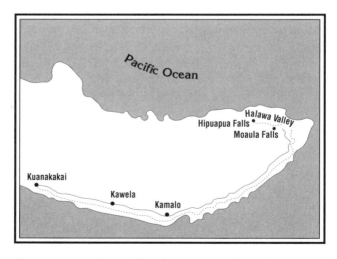

Five more miles will take you to Kamalo, one of Molokai's natural harbors. This was used in the pre-European contact days as a landing for one of the most populated areas on Molokai. It also served in the 19th century as a harbor for small ships carrying cargo along the South Coast. A sugar mill operated in the area and its products were shipped to Honolulu from 1870 to 1900. Later, as the population shifted toward Central Molokai, the shipping center moved to Kanakauki.

The remnants of an ancient pier stand as a reminder of the commerce that used to be conducted here. The distant view of the Pineapple Island of Lanai offers another impressive inter-island panorama.

The first permanent Protestant mission was formed at Kaluaaha in 1832 by the Rev. Harvey Rexford Hitchcock when he and his company were sent from Honolulu by the Sandwich Island Mission. Dedicated in 1844, Molokai's first permanent church was then one of the largest western-style buildings in the Islands. It underwent extensive repairs in 1899, and buttresses were added in 1917. The church was used regularly until the 1940s, but all that is left today are the ruins.

Ironically, one of the major ancient temples was just a stone's throw away. Iliiliopae was dedicated to the Islands' highest gods and staffed by priests who instructed worshippers from all over the island. Many early churches were built on the sites of earlier pagan rituals. This was the site of human sacrifice and legends have it that an evil high chief and his followers sacrificed nine sons of a local resident at one time. The myth tells of the father appealing for justice and the high priest and his followers being destroyed by the storms that ensued.

The small bay of Honouliwai and its little valley illustrate the splendid isolation in which many families spent their lives in the early days. Taro was grown in the rich soil of the valley; the bay, with its surviving fishpond, provided a rich harvest from the sea.

The northern spit of land was the site of bonfires to guide fishermen returning from the sea at night. Today, Hawaiian families still maintain a well-ordered community here.

Up a series of steep hills through what is today cattle country, then down a sharp precipice, is Halawa Valley, the site of the oldest (650 AD) recorded human settlement in Hawaii. It was the home of a large agricultural community until a tsunami struck in 1946, wiping out the local population.

The hike up through the valley to its beautiful waterfalls takes about two hours and is a rewarding excursion for the whole family. The valley is also an idyllic camping spot for visitors to spend a few days.

There are two sets of waterfalls at the end of the valley: Hipuapua Falls and Moaula Falls. Moaula has an upper and lower falls, with a large pool at the base of the lower one. Hipuapua is a single waterfall with a dumbell-shaped pool at its base. The pool under Moaula Falls is large enough for a good swim, with a lot of broad rocks for sunbathing.

From the parking area at the end of the main road, it is easy to get to the trailhead by following the dirt road past the church and a number of houses on both sides of the road. The road ends after about a half-mile and a footpath continues alongside a stone wall on the left for 150 yards. You have to scout for the best place to ford the Halawa Stream here because the brook bed is ever-changing. The trail continues on the other side of the stream through a dense stand of giant mango trees (the fruit is delicious in season).

From the lowland, flat stream, the trail heads into the hills to another path running parallel to the stream. The trail out the fork to the left leads to the falls through thousands of fruit trees and then along a water pipe on the way to the next falls.

Along the way, it passes over, along, and through scores of ancient taro terraces. This was once one of the most productive and fertile agricultural areas in Hawaii. Moaula Falls lies about 100 yards past the north fork of Halawa Stream – a great place for a cool swim.

A little more than 75 yards past the north fork, just before the falls, there is a spur trail that heads off to the right and up the cliff 150 yards before it, too, divides. The trail to the right leads up to the pool at the base of the upper Moaula Falls. The other spur goes through dense brush to Hipuapua Falls. Caution is essential because the trail edges along a nearly vertical way. There is a cable to help climbers, but it is still not for the faint of heart.

The trail to Hipuapua is not well-maintained and rock slides can make it even harder to follow, but the 500-foot falls will reward your efforts. The pool at their base is smaller than Moaula's, but it is still a good place to cool off and relax in nature.

Even though the little island of Molokai has been a popular weekend destination for Honoluluans for years, only recently have other travelers started visiting. That makes it an even more special place. Unlike the large tourist meccas on Oahu, Maui, Kauai, and the Big Island, Molokai will not "come to you." Instead, visitors have to approach it on its own terms. Spectacular scenery and fascinating historic sites abound, and it is still small enough to see everything – certainly by car, but also on foot. If you are looking for a quiet place where it is easy to forget the 20th century, but with plenty of history, and where there are good places for roughing it, then Molokai is for you.

Lanaii

20

Hiking The Pineapple Isle

After six decades as the private Pineapple Island, Lanai has opened to visitors more than just its beaches and pine-studded highlands. Castle & Cooke Inc., owner of Dole Pineapple, is building two hotels, the 250-room Manele at Hulopoe Bay on a dazzling white sand beach, and a 102-room lodge at Koele in the central highlands. The Lodge has been built of heavy timber with beamed ceilings and stone fireplaces rarely seen in Hawaii. The Manele Bay commands the sandy south shore looking across to Maui and its old whaling port of Lahaina.

For an island that ranks only sixth in size among all the Hawaiian Islands, Lanai offers a startling assortment of climates. Shipwreck Beach is a four-mile stretch of sand shaded by kiawe trees and has been a popular strand for live-in beachcombers.

On the other hand, Munro Trail leads to the heights at Lanaipali at 3,400 feet, from which intrepid hikers can catch glimpses of all the major Hawaiian Islands except Kauai. You can hike among the stately Norfolk

Island pines, along a ridge flowering with specimens brought to Hawaii by the gentleman for whom the trail was named.

No other place in the Islands is quite like Lanai City. Located just below the mountains at 1,600 feet above sea level, its climate is like that of a California mountain town in summer. It has a plantation office, school, hospital, several churches, post office, golf courses, bank, a couple of gas stations, café, bakery, courthouse, even a jail – and that's it folks.

It is said by those who know such things that the best preserved and most extensive ancient ruins in the Islands are in Kaunolu Village. The remnants of 86 homes, 35 stone shelters, and various grave markings and garden sites are scattered along a point above the sea.

A National Historic Landmark, Kaunolu was once an active fishing community and a favorite recreation spot for Hawaiian royalty. From here it is possible to hike about two miles along the cliff tops to Pali Kaholo, the highest point on the coastline at 1,000 feet.

SHIPWRECK BEACH TRAIL
Distance: 16 miles
Permit requirements: none
Rating: strenuous family

This particular hike starts out about 10 miles from the Post Office in town. The hiking trail between Shipwreck Beach and Polihua Beach is long and hot, but it is well worth the effort. The entire length on the northeast shore of the island is littered with shipwreckage, ocean debris, and beautiful seashells. The good pickings on this little-visited beach make it a beachcomber's delight. What's more, it is not necessary to hike the entire route.

The trail itself starts on a rocky rise overlooking Kukui Point, at the site of an old light house. All that remains is a cold, concrete slab.

The interesting beach houses near the point of land are built almost completely of timbers from wrecked ships and locally found driftwood. For less intrepid hikers, the walk from Kukui Point to the hulk of a large ship rusting on the rocks about 150 yards offshore is only half a mile, and the round-trip trek takes about an hour.

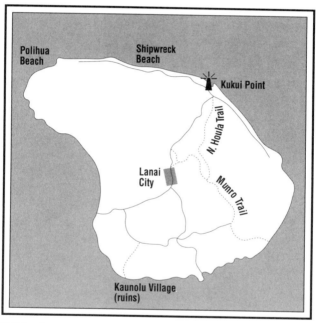

With the exception of Munro Trail, there is no real backpacking on this flat table of an island. Munro Trail into the mountains is really three trails in one, each with its own individual attractions.

MUNRO TRAIL
Distance: 18 miles
Permit requirements: none
Rating: strenuous

The Munro Trail itself begins innocently enough, but try it only on foot. Four-wheel vehicles may be able to get through, but shortly after the trailhead it gets very wet and rutted.

It is named for George C. Munro, a naturalist who reforested this part of Lanai with exotic plants to restore a watershed area. The trail begins about 1½ miles from Lanai City off Keomuku Road.

You begin by climbing up the east side of the mountains, with beautiful views of Maui and Molokai. At the head of Maunalei Gulch, the King of Hawaii massacred many natives of Lanai who sought the valley's refuge.

Beyond the gulch, the trail passes through forests of Norfolk Island pines. These tall trees collect moisture from low-hanging clouds so they were planted to help increase the ground water. There are a lot of flat, grassy spots to camp. Theoretically, permits are required from the State Department of Land and Natural Resources in Lanai City, but this is not seriously enforced.

A trail marker on the left identifies North Hauola Trail at 4½ miles, just before the end of the road, and Lanaihale (house of Lanai) is just past that. There is a good picnic spot with a wonderful view of Lanai City at 5½ miles.

Half a mile farther on, there is a sign for the Hauola Trail, a heavily overgrown, little-used path. From there, the trail makes an abrupt descent with many beautiful views of Maui, Kahoolawe, and the Big

Island of Hawaii. The trail comes to an abrupt stop when you reach the pineapple fields. Bearing right, the main road will lead you back to Lanai City.

NORTH HAUOLA TRAIL
Distance: 4 miles
Permit requirements: none
Rating: strenuous

This is most often recommended as a side hike off the Munro Trail. The prettiest part is the first mile, as far as the impressive eucalyptus grove. Long pants are recommended, however, to avoid scratches from the dense vegetation.

The trail generally follows a ridge line dominated by Norfolk Island pines. On clear days, you can see Oahu, Molokai, Kahoolawe, and sometimes the Big Island of Hawaii.

It is important to be cautious if you walk to the edge of the ridge because both sides are vertical drops. If you are ambitious and want to proceed past the eucalyptus grove you can continue, following a ridge to the right until you reach a beautiful point overlooking Maunalei Gulch. Here you will find the Koolanai jeep road, which will take you to the coast.

KAIHOLENA GULCH TRAIL
Distance: 5½ miles
Permit requirements: none
Rating: strenuous

The best way to get to the trailhead is to drive out Keomuku Road, take the first left, bear right at a fork in the road, and park on a small rise near a grove of

Norfolk Island pines. This is a pleasant mountain hike with some magnificent views to the west side of the little island.

The trail itself follows the pole line up a hill and passes through twin poles at the top of the rise. From there, it swings right through a grove of eucalyptus trees and begins to climb a ridge between Kaiholena Gulch and Hulopoe Gulch. It is in good condition and easy to follow to the Munro Trail Road about a mile away.

In season, the higher reaches of the hike are great places for finding ripe guavas. After the first mile, you turn onto the Munro Trail Road and can enjoy views of the west side of Maui.

Passing a stairway from an abandoned homesite, the trail continues northwest, then turns south to a broad flat area. The trees in this section have been tied with tapes to mark the trail.

Long pants are in order again to avoid scratches from the undergrowth, and care should be exercised at the lookouts because of the near-vertical drops.

The trail continues to the top of the ridge, Puu Alii (which means royal hill), with great views of Lanai City. The northwestern descent starts out gradually enough, but becomes quite steep.

You can continue down the hill through stands of eucalyptus to a point where the trail turns sharply left toward a large satellite dish and a former pineapple field a short distance beyond. Once you reach the old pineapple road, it is an easy hike back into town. Or, more ardent enthusiasts can return back along the trail.

Until the new hotel opened, Hotel Lanai was the place to stay, and so it remains for people who want a taste of the real Lanai. Originally built in the 1920s for Dole's supervisors and guests, it was the only place to stay, unless you planned to camp. Today, the charming 10-room inn nestled in Norfolk Island pines has been completely restored. Even if you are enjoying Lanai only for a day's outing, this is a great place to stop for refreshments.

Hawaii

21

Waipio Valley & Mauna Kea

Near the northernmost point of the Big Island of Hawaii, there is a special place called Waipio. Once the home of 50,000 Hawaiians and later of President John F. Kennedy's first Peace Corps training camp, today it is a remote and little-visited place which modern man has forgotten – and nature has reclaimed.

Towering high above Waipio is the often snow-capped peak of Mauna Kea, hosting the greatest concentration of astronomical observatories on earth. Peering 14 billion light years into space from here, astronomers are changing our view of the universe, how it evolved, and our place in it.

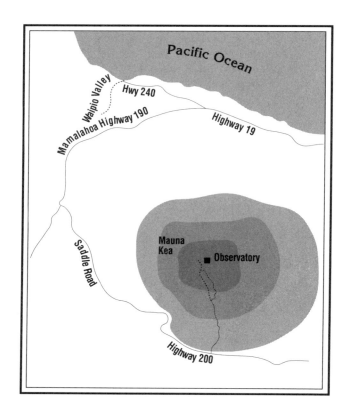

WAIPIO VALLEY
Distance: 5 miles
Permit requirements: Kamehameha
School Bishop Estate
Rating: difficult

When experienced hikers dream of Hawaii, they picture Kipahulu Valley on Maui, the Kalalau Trail on Kauai, and Waipio on the Big Island. These are true wilderness experiences.

The first view of Waipio Valley comes at the end of Highway 240 where there is a scenic lookout into the dramatic green gorge. The 2,000-foot gouge in the earth is one of the great panoramas of the Islands, competing, perhaps, with the Nuuanu Pali on Oahu.

The only ways to enter the valley are on foot or by four-wheel-drive vehicle, although the latter should only be tried by an expert.

The valley floor was important in early Hawaii. Fertile land and plentiful water made a rich life possible centuries before the arrival of European man. The first Western people visited Waipio in 1823 and reported a thriving agricultural community. Later, Chinese immigrants settled there, and stayed until the U.S. Government closed the school system in the 1930s. The Peace Corps reopened the valley in the 1960s and the remnants of their camp are hardly visible today. Now, only a handful of tenacious taro farmers remain, preserving a way of life that disappeared generations ago.

The trail begins at a 900-foot perch with a dramatic panorama into the lush valley. In the distance, hikers get their first glimpse of two 2,000-foot waterfalls plunging into the valley floor.

The jeep road ends about a mile into the valley. From there it is possible to head out to the black sand beach or back up into the valley where the original community stood. Where Waipio Stream empties into the sea you will discover one of the Big Island's most unforgettable black sand beaches and one of its best spots for picnicking.

Follow the stream up into the valley and you will find some rewarding sights. The falls are not always "turned on," however, since the sugar company uses the water for irrigation. Two miles upstream you reach the base of the falls, but the surrounding vegetation is thick and can be virtually impassable. Perhaps the most beautiful sight is the blanket of impatiens blossoms all around the trail and covering the entire valley floor. It is possible to continue on another 12 miles into Waimanu, a smaller valley up the coast, but this requires the commitment of at least a full day.

THE SNOWS OF MAUNA KEA
Distance: 12 miles
Permit requirements: none
Rating: difficult

High above the seaside valley is the mighty summit of Mauna Kea, but the climb to Hawaii's highest point is not as difficult as it might appear. There are both a hiking trail and a jeep road to the observatories at the peak.

It is important to plan carefully, however, because the trip must be made in a single day. There are no shelters and no camping is allowed at the top. It is also important to check the weather because the slopes are often covered with snow – offering the only chance for skiing in this tropical paradise.

Most visitors to the Big Island think first of volcanoes. People who live in Hawaii, however, know Mauna Kea has represented the state's leading edge in space age technology since President Richard M. Nixon closed the Peace Corps training center in Waipio, and the Apollo moon mission astronauts returned to earth by way of Hawaii.

NASA had even more important plans for the Big Island when the snow-capped 14,000-foot peak of Mauna Kea was selected as the site for the space agency's night-time astronomical observatory. Today, the observatory offers a view of most of the southern and northern night skies and 92% of all the stars visible from earth.

The altitude and absence of air pollution and urban light have conspired to make it the best spot for peering into space. Most other sites in North America and Europe are deteriorating rapidly because urban development is flooding the skies with man-made light that interferes with the view. But the skies of Mauna Kea remain clear.

Because of the near-perfection of the Mauna Kea location, scientists from all over the world, including France, the Netherlands, Great Britain, Japan, and Canada in addition to the U.S. have selected this as the site of their nations' telescopes. Today the world's investments in these advanced pieces of equipment have exceeded $500 million, representing the greatest star-gazing capacity at any one site on earth.

The telescopes are not the only things for hikers to see atop Mauna Kea. This may be the only place in the world where it is possible to walk from an orchid-lined path through a dense rainforest at sea level to a scene of lunar-like desolation above the clouds in a single day.

The scientists of the National Park Service have done an outstanding job of bringing into cultivation the upper-elevation flora at the national parks on Mauna Kea, as at Haleakala on Maui, where the magnificent silversword plants are no longer endangered thanks to their efforts. Native birds, including the state bird (the nene goose) and the palila, thrive at the higher elevations of these two specacular parks.

In many ways, however, the mid-elevation open woodland through which you pass is the most interesting ecological niche. It is here, without the Federal protection of the upper-elevation parks, that the rarest and most endangered species of native plants are to be found, in a precarious ecological balance with wildlife – especially feral pigs and goats.

There is rich archeological evidence that early man also hiked to the upper levels of Mauna Kea. Generally, Polynesians settled near the sea, but they prayed to many gods, especially for protection from the powerful natural forces they so feared. It is not difficult to picture prehistoric man cowering in fear at the exploding earth, with fire shooting into the air and molten lava pouring down the mountainside. Today much of Northern Hawaii is a wasteland of lava such eruptions left behind.

A survey of the plateau region of the volcano has turned up 20 shrines in an area of approximately 1,000 acres. Whatever their purpose, they are unique in the entire Pacific Basin and nothing else has been discovered at comparable elevations anywhere.

Standing among these primitive shrines of ancient man, yet beholding the space-age astronomical observatories that share the mountain, it is impossible not to be profoundly moved. This is one of the few places on earth where you can stand in one place and see man's entire journey, from his most primitive beginnings, bowing before unknown gods, to his leap off the planet and into the vast reaches of outer space.

22

The Kona-Kohala Coast

THE KONA-KOHALA TRAIL
Distance: 37 miles
Permit requirements: none
Rating: family

The lower slopes of Mauna Kea below the national park and the rest of the northern part of the Big Island are dominated by the 230,000-acre Parker Ranch, the largest single farm holding in the United States. It has recently opened to the public, though hiking is still not permitted in the ranch. The road down the windward coast to Kailua-Kona, however, offers a long, safe hike and the chance to see some unique historic sites. Start out early because the hike is long and dry. Also, there are few places to overnight between the luxury hotels in the north and the village of Kailua-Kona.

What you see today are the remnants of major ancient structures and, in some places, their partially restored remains. Nowhere is the Hawaiian heritage from ancient times richer than along the Kona-Kohala Coast of the Big Island of Hawaii, and there is no better way to discover it than on foot.

Native Hawaiians trace their past through oral geneology, chanted down from generation to generation. The verbal records suggest that one of the oldest and largest heiaus (ancient temples) on the island was built about 480 AD, more than 1,000 years before the arrival of Captain James Cook.

There were different kinds of heiau which served several purposes. These ancient places of worship

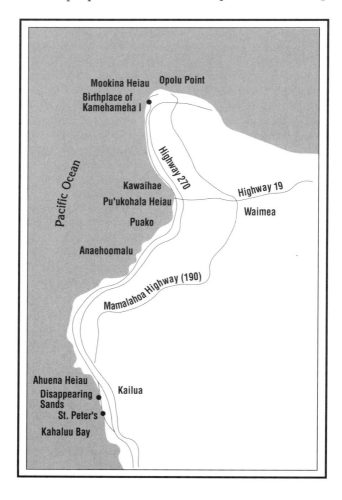

were usually built of lava rock to form foundations, walls and altars. The temples themselves were all destroyed upon the death of Kamehameha I in 1819 when his widow and his son, the new king, broke the old religious kapu, or system of religious prohibitions.

Mookina Luakini Heiau is located in the North Kohala district, near the northernmost tip of the Big Island. This magnificent temple was dedicated to one of the four most powerful gods in Polynesian Hawaii: Kunuiakea, the god the ancients turned to for rain and growth, for fishing and sorcery, and, most of all, for strength in war.

Worshippers, including kings and the ruling chiefs (alii nui), used this temple for human sacrifice, confinement in preparation for major battles, praying, and fasting. It is said to have been at this point that the early Hawaiians studied the rain and wind as omens of the dark world around them.

Tradition also has it that the 30-foot walls were built in a single night. The water-worn basalt used in its construction was passed from hand to hand along a human chain of 20,000 men spanning 14 miles from the Pololu Valley to the north.

In 1963, Mookini Luakini Heiau was made a National Historic Landmark. It was one of the most sacred sites in pre-contact Hawaii, and today is the only temple still cared for by a direct descendant of the long line of kahunas (priests or experts) designated in ancient times.

The nearby birth site of Kamehameha I, also known as "The Great" because he was the first chieftain to unite all the Islands, is also a National Historic Landmark. The Mookini family geneology chant holds that his birth rituals were performed at this incredible heiau, and that he used it until he rebuilt Puukohola Heiau, 17 miles to the south in Kawaihae.

The naturally sheltered harbor of Kawaihae was an important stopping-off point for early European visitors. It was also the principal residence of Kamehameha I from 1790 to 1794, and it was where he regrouped his warriors and prepared for the battles to conquer his island kingdom.

Tradition also has it that he rebuilt or expanded Puukohola, a massive temple of war, at about that time. It was described by an early missionary as having a wall 20 feet high and six feet wide on one side and as being about 225 feet long and 100 feet wide. It has been restored today to reflect those dimensions.

At the dedication of Puukohola Kamehameha I sacrificed his archrival and cousin, Koua Kuahuula, for plotting against him. By 1795, the first king had conquered all the islands except Kauai to the north – Maui, Molokai, Kahoolawe, and Oahu.

Petroglyphs are among the earliest human artifacts left – pictures chipped into the lava rocks by ancient artists. The Big Island has the largest concentration of petroglyph sites in Hawaii; they are limited almost exclusively to this Kona-Kohala Coast. Anaehoomalu on the Kaniku lava flow in the Waikoloa area has a spectacular concentration of petroglyphs. There is a wide variety of complex forms, from human figures to abstractions.

Nearby, the so-called Mamalahoa Highway which crosses the Kaniku flow, is a fine example of the horse trails built during the mid-19th century for riders traveling up and down the lava-covered coast. Today, it proves a convenient alternative for hikers who want to avoid the broad highway shoulders designed to do double service as trails. A few miles to the north is another of the three or four major petroglyph sites in the archipelago of Hawaii.

Puako, located near picturesque Puako Bay, has more than 3,000 images, including birth scenes, marching figures and one believed to represent Lono, the god of the harvest. There are indications that these are the oldest petroglyphs in Hawaii.

Another heiau, located between Kawaihae Bay and Puukohola, is said to have been dedicated to Lono. Mailekinni Heiau, which has been partially restored, is roughly the size of a football field, with six-foot walls. More recently, the U.S. Army has used it as an observation post. Today, it is protected as part of the Puukohola Heiau complex.

On the northern side of Kawaihai Bay is another heiau, which was partially submerged when the harbor was built. The little heiau called Hale o Kapuni is said to have been used by Kamehameha I.

Even today, you can watch the sharks come in every evening to feed here. It is said that this time-honored custom began because the ancients fed the dangerous fish they so revered.

There was another significant temple used by Kamehameha I, which at the time adjoined the king's residence, called Kamakahonu. This stands in the Niumalu Bay, now called Kailua, and it is where he died.

The Hulihee Palace overlooks Kailua Bay just across from another luakini (or sacrificial, including the human variety) temple and the home of the war god. Today, the palace has been restored in memory of the era when the royal family lived in Kailua-Kona, and it marks a fitting end to the long hike down the coast.

Commissioned by the first governor of Hawaii, John Kuakini, this two-storey Victorian village centerpiece was built in 1838. Its English country-manor architecture is another indication of the reverence the

Hawaiian monarchy had for things British, and it is the best starting point for any walk around town.

In the 1880s, King David Kalakaua used the home as his summer palace. Featuring 19th-century furnishings, it is now a museum restored to the magnificence of the Kalakaua period.

The palace is filled with relics of the days when the royal family lived and vacationed here. The simple coral and lava walls of the palace house some of the most priceless artifacts of the monarchy.

King Kamehameha I spent his final ruling years in Kailua, and a recreation of his royal palace grounds can be found north of the seawall on a tiny peninsula adjacent to the hotel named for him. Known as Kamakahonu, this was also the site of the feast marking the overthrow of the religious kapu system in 1819.

The busy Kailua Pier sits between that peninsula and the Hulihee Palace in the village itself. It is the embarkation point for fishing trips, snorkeling and diving excursions, and submarine tours. Usually one of the three interisland ferries can be seen anchored just beyond the pier in the large bay.

Kailua Village has come to be dominated by shops, cafés, restaurants and night spots, somewhat in the spirit of Provincetown or Monterey. It is a special spot for walking tours, but there is more to see than the historic Hulihee Palace and the stores.

Directly across Alii Drive from the palace stands the oldest church in the Hawaiian Islands, Mokuaikaua. Completed in 1837 by the first company of missionaries, the church has rock walls mortared with coral, and hand-hewn ohia beams more than 50 feet long joined by wooden pins – no iron nails for this construction project.

Two spreading monkeypod trees on Alii Drive frame another church at the south end of the village, St. Michael's. It was completed in 1848 on the site of the first Catholic mission in the Neighbor Islands.

Alii Drive stretches south of the little village for five miles to the posh resort of Keauhou. The entire route is popular with both hikers and bikers. Disappearing Sands Beach may be the most interesting spot for swimming. It is the only beach in the Islands that disappears every day, and reappears again.

One of the most historic sights south of the village is the blue and white St. Peter's Catholic Church at Kahaluu Bay. About the size of a playhouse, it was built on the site of an ancient heiau to combat superstition, but of late it has been the target of repeated desecration.

Still more heiaus and petroglyphs can be discovered in the Kona Gardens. This botanical and cultural park is also a great place to buy fresh local fruit and vegetables every Saturday morning if you are planning a longer stay.

At the end of the road a wondrous view down the coast beckons, but since 1983 it has tended to be heavily shrouded with clouds that can choke visitors who have respiratory problems. This "vog," a phenomenon unique to the Islands of Hawaii, is caused by the gaseous and ash emissions from Kilauea, the most active volcano on earth.

23

Climbing Kilauea

Distance: 18 miles
Permit requirements: none
Rating: family

Hawaii's not-to-be-missed spectacle is Kilauea, the world's only "hike through" volcano and one that offers the spectacle of frequent, easily-accessible eruptions. The walk around Crater Rim Drive males you want to reach out and touch the process of creation taking place before your eyes.

Kilauea is the best known and most popular of the Big Island's attractions. Every day hikers come in the hope of witnessing Pele, the volcano goddess, in one of her outbursts. She is unpredictable and may not be giving her best performance on the day of any particular visit. However, over the past five years, she has been more likely than not to be putting on an act unlike anything you might expect.

Mountains spewing fire and red hot ash into the sky and glowing flows of molten lava are awesome to behold, but, even at its tamest, Hawaii's Volcanoes National Park is a fascinating place to go hiking. Two of the world's rare live volcanoes, Kilauea and Mauna Loa, lie within its 350 square miles.

Established in 1916, the park includes the summit caldera and the upper northeast flank of Mauna Loa, the Kilauea caldera, with its southern and eastern flanks, and a stretch of the Puna Coast at Kalapuna with its eerie volcanic landscape, rainforest, and rare birds and plant life – all easily seen on foot.

The park, 30 miles southwest of Hilo, has two entrances and can be reached by Highway 11 or 13. Both have visitor centers stocked with booklets on the volcanoes, plants and wildlife, plus map-guides for hiking. Mauna Loa stretches out of the sea almost 14,000 feet to its summit. Kilauea is 4,000 feet above sea level. Unlike the sudden explosions of volcanoes elsewhere, such as Mt. St. Helens, these eruptions are less violent. But the lava flows continuously, forming rivers, falls, and lakes with spectacular fountains of fire. They are so accessible, you can usually get close-up view.

Sometimes the erupting lava from Mauna Loa stays within Mokuaweoweo, the summit caldera. Usually, however, it spills over and down the slopes and runs out of rifts in the mountainside far below the summit.

Kilauea Volcano, however, is the real show stopper, and Halemaumau, its huge crater-within-a-crater (over two miles in diameter), is the firepit the goddess Pele is said now to call home. Its main vent is less than a mile wide and its depth changes constantly as the lava ebbs and flows. Sometimes it erupts in the sky with bursts of scarlet lava, but in quieter times you can walk to the edge and look down into the hot core of the earth.

After more than a century of bubbling and sometimes overflowing its lava lakebed, the volcano went silent in 1924 after a series of steam gas explosions. But

Kilauea's continuous eruptions in the last five years have more than made up for its nap.

Lava flowing down the hills has repeatedly destroyed the road and every home in its way. It frequently reaches the sea, where it has created hundreds of acres of the newest land on earth and the largest black sand beach on the Big Island of Hawaii.

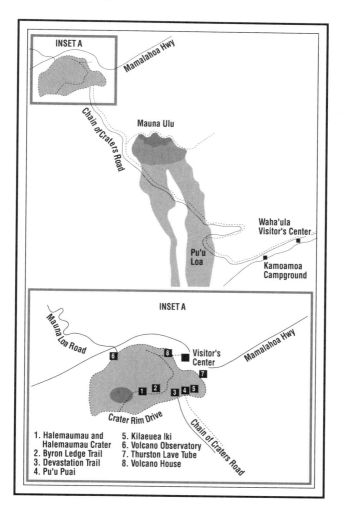

Hikers (without respiratory difficulties) can walk the 11-mile Crater Rim Drive from the Kilauea Visitor Center around and into the summit caldera, across both rift zones, and over a bleak desert impossible to imagine without seeing it. There is a special feel to the lava flows on Kilauea and up and down the Windward Coast, a splendid desolation that is awesome.

Before or after the trek, you should stop at Volcano House, located directly across the street from the visitor center. This hunting lodge sitting right on the lip of Kilauea crater offers 37 rooms looking into the volcano. It also has a warm and wonderful sitting room off the lobby with a large ohia wood fire on chilly evenings, and a glassed terrace for volcano watching. You always have to remember it is usually cool in the upper elevations of Hawaii.

There is a 3½-mile, self-guiding Halemaumau Trail that starts near Volcano House and crosses the scarred and scorched floor of the Kilauea caldera to the rim of Halemaumau. This is probably the park's most popular hiking route and it offers some dramatic views. You should try to set out early, before the sun bakes the floor of the crater. It is easy to walk back along the 3½-mile Byron Ledge Trail or to arrange a ride to Volcano House.

There is more to see in the park, although the volcano is the most spectacular. The current Volcano House was actually built in 1941, and part of the original 1877 building was moved across the street adjacent to the visitor center. It now houses the Volcano Art Center, with first-class works inspired by the volcanoes on display.

You can hike or drive up the Mauna Loa Strip Road, a side route up the mountain to an overlook and shelter at the start of the 18-mile trail to Mokuaweoweo. It is a long climb, but there is a lot to see, including a bird park, and an oasis in the lava where the flow was parted by the earth. The panoramic view from the top on a clear day makes it well worth the effort.

It is possible to continue around Crater Rim Drive to the Kilauea Overlook, a good spot for a picnic on the edge of the vast, lava-scorched depression. A half-mile farther on is the Hawaiian Volcano Observatory, located on the high point of the crater's west wall. This is operated by the U.S. Geological Survey and is the only research program aimed at developing a better understanding of volcanic behavior, with the goal of predicting eruptions. Hikers are always welcomed by the scientists in charge.

From the halfway point on Crater Rim Drive, there is a short trail to the Halemaumau Overlook right on its crumbling (but safe) lip. The depth of the drop-off and geological formations you see will depend on the most recent activity of the volcano.

When it is open, Devastation Trail is an incredible half-mile boardwalk over cinders. It takes you through the skeletal remains of a forest wiped out by the volcanic eruptions of 1959. As always, the lunar-like lava-covered land is fascinating, but so is the sight of the vegetation beginning the rebirth of a fertile land.

Puu Puai straddles Kilauea Iki (little Kilauea), a 400-foot cone of ash and pumice formed by a dazzling 1959 eruption when the volcano shot its lava 2,000 feet up into the air. The Kilauea Iki Trail leads hikers across the floor of the chasm and, as on Devastation Trail, the creative force of nature is at work as fern and ohia plants are starting to grow through the crater's cracks.

At the easternmost point of Crater Rim Drive is the 450-foot-long, 10-foot-high Thurston Lava Tube, formed when an ancient lava flow hardened, while molten lava continued to run through it. Although this is one of the largest, lava tubes are relatively common phenomena in Hawaii.

Countless hikes are also possible along Chain of Craters Road, a 27-mile drive from Kilauea Crater at the 4,000-foot mark to the sea along the 90-mile road back to Hilo. There are three active fault "escarpments" here, edges of the Eastern Rift Zone, and the smoldering base of Mauna Ulu (growing mountain), a 385-foot volcanic cone built up by the eruptions.

Near the coastal junction of the Chain of Craters Road with Highway 130, there is another trailhead at Puu Loa. The Old Puna-Kau Trail stretches about a half-mile east to a wealth of petroglyph mounds in the Park's Kalapana Section.

The Kamoamoa Campground on the coast overlooking an arch, created when wave action eroded a lava tube, offers another good center for hiking and water sports. The rock walls spreading in every direction outline an ancient village compound and the partially restored remnants of Moa Heiau.

Next to the Wahaula Visitor Center at the park's Kalapana entrance are the ruins of Wahaula Heiau. One of the oldest ancient temples in the islands, it was built in about 1250 AD by Tahitian priests who are thought to have introduced the severe religious system of human sacrifice and kapu which was practiced until 1819.

From the summit of Kilauea, Highway 11 descends to the Kau Desert on the volcano's southwest slope. From there it heads toward the historic sites of the Kona-Kohala Coast.

Just before leaving the national park, there is a trail called Mauna Iki (footprints). It leads to a battlefield where soldiers fighting Kamehameha I for control of the Big Island were asphyxiated by fumes and dust from the eruption of Halemaumau. The event led

Hawaiians to conclude that the great volcano goddess Pele interceded on behalf of Kamehameha, which certainly enhanced his prestige as he went on to unite all the major islands save Kauai. You can continue on the Mauna Iki Trail a mile to a dome that belched gases from the volcano in 1920, creating Great Crack, a massive fissure extending to the sea. Lava foundations broke out here again in 1971 and should remind you of the care needed as you explore Hawaii on foot.

There is an overwhelming feeling to the Islands, here on Kilauea and in a thousand other places where you can see their awesome beauty. As usual, Mark Twain probably put it best.

"No... land in all the world has any deep strong charm for me but that one; no other land could so longingly and beseechingly haunt me sleeping and waking through half a lifetime, as that one has done. Other things leave me but it abides; other things change but it remains the same. For me its balmy airs are always blowing, its summer seas flashing in the sun, the pulsing of its surf-beat in my ear; I can see its garlanded crags; its leaping cascades, its plumy palms drowsing by the shore; its remote summits floating like islands above the cloud rack; I can feel the spirit of its woodland solitudes; I can hear the splash of its brooks; in my nostrils still lives the breath of flowers that perished twenty years ago."

A vacation in Hawaii is an experience you too will never forget. Perhaps that is why locals call it "No Ka Oi!" for that means "no place better."

Index